" And behold, there was a great earthquake, for the Angel of the Lord descended from heaven, and came and rolled back the stone from the door, and sat upon it. His countenance was like lightning, and his raiment white as snow. And for fear of him, the keepers did shake, and became as dead men."—MATTHEW XXVIII, 2, 3, 4.

A

HAND BOOK

FOR THE

𝕬𝖑𝖇𝖆𝖓𝖞 𝕽𝖚𝖗𝖆𝖑 𝕮𝖊𝖒𝖊𝖙𝖊𝖗𝖞,

WITH AN

APPENDIX ON EMBLEMS.

By EDWARD FITZGERALD.

ALBANY:
VAN BENTHUYSEN PRINTING HOUSE.
1871.

1

HINTS TO THE VISITOR.

AS we deem it superfluous to apologize to you—
especially if it happens that you are a stranger to
these highly diversified grounds, with their weirdly
wrought net work of serpentine avenues and paths,
so perfectly bewildering in the intensity of its
complication—for introducing to you this little
manual, and recommending it as an intelligent and
agreeable companion for a ramble among the Silent,
we will lose but little time in proceeding to ex-
plain how you may avail yourself of its services to
the best advantage.

We imagine that if, upon the occasion of your
first visit, you undertake to explore the Albany
Rural Cemetery entirely unassisted, you will find
the task to involve a geographical puzzle about as
intricate as any that can easily be condensed within
the limits of two hundred and thirty acres. Now,
permit us to show you how this puzzle can be
quietly unraveled without the aid of an obtrusive
or garrulous instructor.

In the first place we would suggest a look at the
map that nestles just inside the nether cover of
this book. A single glance will discover to you
that the occupied portions of the grounds are sub-
divided (nature herself has made three grand
divisions) into a great many numbered sections,
each one of which is circumscribed by a road or
roads. It is obviously unnecessary to inform you

that these subdivisions are intended to facilitate
the finding of any particular spot or object that
you may wish to reach.

You will readily conceive that you can locate
the vicinity of whatever you desire to find much
easier by knowing what section it is in than by
being told that it is on such or such an avenue,
path, ridge or hill. An avenue or path may be of
considerable length, and may bound upon one side
or run through a number of sections. So it is evi-
dent that such a clue is comparatively indefinite.

Then, again, the names of these upon the map
may defy your closest scrutiny for a time, while a
section number—particularly here for the numbers
are very regular—will be quickly discovered.

Having given you a general idea of the utility
of the section system, let us now request you to
examine the map more minutely. In some part
of every section you will notice a small cross. The
significance of this and one of its uses we will ex-
plain by illustration, as follows: Suppose that in
wandering over the grounds you become bewildered
and lose all knowledge of your location and of the
points of the compass. In trying to untangle
the snarl, in your judgment, you are moving along
at random, when your attention is attracted by a
low wooden post near the roadside surmounted by
an iron cap which bears the abreviation " Sec." and
the number—we will say, 100. You look at your
map and find section 100. The cross or obelisk in
that section shows the exact location of the post at
your feet.

By this reference your absolute as well as your
relative position is immediately determined, the
kinks are nicely smoothed out of your organ of

locality, and off you go to—again get lost perhaps, and again to consult your undeviating land mark. You can never go far without finding it, as the sections are generally small, and each one is designated by a section post conspicuously placed.

As to the superiority of the plan we have adopted in this manual with a view to giving you a good general idea of the beauties of the Cemetery, without unnecessary travel or loss of time, opinions may differ. The *Tour* is the popular route (for carriages at least), but its appropriation does not suit our present purpose.

Nature, as we have said, has made three grand divisions of the grounds, which are known respectively as the *North Ridge*, the *South Ridge* and the *Middle Ridge* and we have concluded, in this instance, to take the cue from Nature by marking out a distinct route for each division.

This plan we consider the best for the guidance of a person unfamiliar with the grounds. He will be less liable to lose his bearings than if he follows the mystifying *Tour*, and his interest in the attractions will not be diluted by the reflection that he has crossed and recrossed the same ravine and has been on and off the same ridge several times during his erratic journey.

After you have become acquainted with the grounds by the means we have indicated, we fancy you will find that a trip around the *Tour* will admit of pleasurable repetition more frequently than if you had chosen this superficial route upon the occasion of your first visit, thereby skimming off the cream of attraction too rapidly for mental assimilation.

You will probably infer from the tone of our
1*

greeting that we are exclusively enlisted in the service of "The man who walks." If so, your surmises are well founded, for, in our humble opinion, the person who thoroughly enjoys the "contemplative recreation" to be found within the limits of an extensive Rural Cemetery—that school of instruction, as a celebrated writer has called it, in architecture, sculpture, landscape gardening, arboriculture and botany—is in this connection essentially peripatetic.

The pedestrian only will find a short cut to an inviting eminence by mounting its acclivitous side. He will monopolize the privilege of traversing moss-clad ravines, whose perennial streams seem specially made to soften the midsummer's heat for his particular benefit. Many an extra "sermon in stones" will be read to him, many a chaste little gem of emblematic sculpture, that is rendered doubly interesting from its sequestered situation—from the disposition evinced to hide it away from unsympathizing scrutiny—will whisper to him of true love, or grief, or lasting remembrance, which a carriage ride will not reveal.

If you desire to obtain a good knowledge of what the Albany Rural Cemetery contains, we recommend that you devote at least two days to the object. An exploration of the *SOUTH RIDGE* alone, if you simply use the means of locomotion that were born with you, will probably give you sufficient physical and mental exercise for one day. Then the *MIDDLE* and *NORTH RIDGES* might successively be traversed upon the occasion of your next visit.

If you should prefer to ride you can, of course, accomplish the entire trip—although, no doubt,

with less satisfaction—in a single effort. If, in
either riding or walking, you should choose to pick
out a route of your own you will still find this
manual useful, as its index will refer you to the
page upon which you can see some allusion to any
prominent object that attracts your attention. The
perusal of this will also indicate to you the Sections
in which lie many of the illustrious dead who are
interred in the Cemetery.

Here it seems proper to mention, that in the
preparation of this little companion for the visitor,
we are indebted to the courtsey of several Albany
gentlemen for data concerning the noted person-
ages referred to. The valuable works of Mr. Joel
Munsell have also been consulted, and have afforded
pertinent information that was not otherwise ac-
cessible.

CYPRESS

Lith of G. W. Lewis 452 Broadway, Albany

ESS WATER.

THE ALBANY RURAL CEMETERY.

SOUTH RIDGE.

IT is totally unnecessary to give, even to the most perfect stranger, any specific directions for reaching the Albany Rural Cemetery. The grounds are located with sufficient precision when we tell you that they will be found not far from the western banks of the Hudson, about midway between the universally known and flourishing cities of Albany and Troy.

Almost any resident child ten years of age, in either of the places named, can inform you how to find the outer gate on the Watervliet turnpike; and assuming that you have already arrived there, we will request the pleasure of accompanying you through the splendid avenue that leads to the principal entrance.

Here we strike the *Tour*, which bends to the northwest just beyond the Superintendent's office.

A few steps up this winding slope and we meet an avenue that diverges to the southwest, called *MOUNT WAY*—an avenue that is destined to open up to us the internal grandeur of the *SOUTH RIDGE*, to which division of the grounds we have already commenced to pay our respects.

But let us stop here a moment for a quiet survey of the initial attractions. In the first place, the neatly arranged foregrounds will receive an unspoken compliment, and then we will turn our attention to the monuments which flank them on the west.

Immediately in front of us stands the granite obelisk of MOSES PATTEN, while away to the right, rearing its lofty head high up among the trees, we see a massive shaft ornamented by a medallion head. That is the memorial of JOEL RATHBONE, and enjoys the distinction of being the most ponderous monument upon the grounds. You will scarcely realize from this distance that its size is more than ordinary, but if at any time you should feel disposed to ascend to the elevation upon which it stands for a closer view, you will decide with us that it is no small affair.

As we are still standing in front of the PATTEN monument, we will take advantage of this favorable opportunity to call your attention to a plain illustration of the system of sectioning now in operation here. On either side of the road you will notice a low section post—a feature of which we have already spoken in our "Hints." That one on the easterly division of the foregrounds shows, by the character on its face, that it designates Section Two. You perceive at once that Section Two consists of a portion of ground defined in its outlines by certain roads of the Cemetery, and naturally infer that the extent of every other section is similarly determined. This system was chosen and applied by Superintendent J. P. Thomas, during the year 1870.

Now let us resume our ramble. Turning into *MOUNT WAY* we pass HOYT and VAN SCHAICK, and immediately find ourselves facing the stately free-stone of STEPHEN ALDEN. At the time of its erection this was considered the finest freestone monument on the grounds. Bending round ALDEN northerly, still in *MOUNT WAY*, we pass the neat lot of A. WELLS, and on the opposite side we see a low monument, which, if for no other reason, is worthy of notice for having been the first granite structure erected in the Cemetery. It commemorates THOS. HILLHOUSE, who died ten years before the incorporation of the Cemetery Association. At that time the greater portion of what is now the *SOUTH RIDGE* was a part of the farm of Mr. HILLHOUSE. This portion of the grounds was subsequently deeded to the Association by his heirs; and the old gentleman, who was first buried outside the Cemetery, was finally brought here to stay. His son, JOHN HILLHOUSE, who still lives, was one of the first surveyors of this institution.

Passing the lot of WELLS and ADAMS, we meet the handsome BLEECKER freestone. Here let us call your attention to an unpretending lot just north of BLEECKER, which is surrounded by an iron fence lined with low evergreens. That is where THUR-LOW WEED expects, eventually, to find lasting repose from the cares and excitement of public life. You see that here he is not inclined for display—a peculiarity frequently found in men of his calibre.

Now we pass SLINGERLAND, and the pretty monument of GREGORY on the eminence before us, is seen. On the circular lot above and beyond the GREGORY monument stands the memorial of JARED L. RATHBONE, in design a counterpart of the Tomb of SCIPIO.

Here *MOUNT WAY* takes an abrupt turn to the southwest, and, after leading us up a steep grade past the monuments of HARRIS and NEWLAND and JAMES McCLURE, again sweeps suddenly in the opposite direction. We follow its windings and, passing the memorials of Dr. GANNON and E. E. KENDRICK, find ourselves standing upon the north side of a richly carved Gothic pedestal surmounted by a figure of Faith. This is WM. H. DE WITT's monument—an object that we will

2

contemplate with pleasure for a moment before turning northerly into the *Tour*, which meets us here.*

Now if you feel disposed to leave us and follow the southerly divergence of the *Tour*, we will tell you something beforehand of the principal objects that will meet your eye. In passing between DE WITT and the modest monument of ISAAC W. VOSBURGH, you will stop a second time to admire the former, and will certainly commend the harmonious proportions and substantial appearance of the latter. You will also probably recognize in the names mentioned, that is if you are well informed concerning the existing prominent men of Albany, two gentlemen who have long been among the Trustees of the Cemetery Association. Then you will leave SAFFORD behind and, bending round VOSBURGH to the west, will see successively the names of WISWALL, IRA JAGGER and P. McNAUGHTON, while almost directly back of the two last the monuments of DURANT and WATSON will appear. Farther on will be seen the vault of ARTEMUS FISH and that of the VAN BENTHUYSEN

---

* Where the coherency of the general narrative is broken by a paragraph or more in smaller type, a deviation from the continuous route is indicated. No digression is made unless warranted by the attractions of the avenue, path or road into which it leads you. If this inducement prompts you to deviate, we will be obliged to wait here for you until you have satisfied your curiosity, retraced your steps, and rejoined us at the point of departure. If you wish to adhere strictly to our continuous route, you have simply to skip the matter in small type and to defer, for the present, an inspection of the objects mentioned therein.

WOSBURGH

family. In the latter, now surrounded by representatives of six generations, are the remains of OBADIAH R. VAN BENTHUYSEN, the first to successfully attach steam power to the printing press of America. The experiment in New York resulted in failure, and the project was abandoned, but Mr. VAN BENTHUYSEN soon solved the difficulties, and gave to Albany the credit of enlisting the weird power of steam, in behalf of the progress of civilization in this country that the press has ever been the first to lead. Following on we come to the monuments of JAMES D. WASSON, W. D. STEWART, JAMES RICHARDSON, CROCKER, and the low substantial freestone of S. M. FISH. Next come the monuments of J. P. WILSON, WM. V. MANY, C. MILLER and WOOD, and beyond is the vault of CATHARINE HAMILTON about which some incredible stories are told. Opposite are D. WOODWORTH and J. W. CRANNELL, and then the handsome DAVIDSON memorial will attract your attention.

You will shortly approach one of the most attractive lots on the ground; but before reaching it you will notice the names of N. ROGERS, CALLENDER, D. SMITH, EDWARD JAMES, SHONTS, READ, CRAPO, and the several neat brown headstones in the GRANT lot.

The three marble structures next ahead, in the lot of MONTEATH and HOWES, are those whose effect we have just been anticipating. There are many more expensive memorials here, but few more chaste and suggestive. The first is surmounted by a well executed figure of Grief. The elaborate drapery and floral embellishments of the second will challenge your admiration, and you will read an impressive lesson in the third—the pretty headstone that commemorates "GEORGIE." That life-like little figure in the flower-crowned niche explains itself,—the right hand holds a book, and upon the back of the left rests a butterfly, an emblem of a short life.

16

Now emerging from *MOUNT WAY* northeasterly
into the *TOUR,* we curve round SAMUEL CRAW-
FORD, and see a short distance ahead a cottage
monument of Italian marble, with a medallion
head; and in the same lot a granite sarcophagus.
These are the memorials of the BENEDICTS—father
and son. We will advance towards them, passing
the monuments of WM. SMITH, S. VAN SCHAICK,
and WICKES. We are now on *MOUNT OLIVET.*

That truthful medallion, by Palmer, represents
LEWIS BENEDICT, the elder, who, in his day, was
distinguished for his unselfish zeal in promoting
public welfare, and who enjoyed the intimate
acquaintance and profound respect of many of the
master spirits of his time. A character of no less
note than Horace Greeley, speaks of him as
follows:

"When I first met LEWIS BENEDICT (in 1837)
he was more than fifty years old. Directness,
shrewdness, quickness of observation and inflexible
decision, were his leading characteristics. He was
eminently and emphatically a man of business.

He used no more words than were necessary, and having formed and expressed his opinion was not easily moved to reconsider the matter. His interest in public affairs was profound and eager; but he had no desire to be conspicuous even in movements which he inspired and directed. He had no dream of ever holding office, no wish to be known as a wielder of authority or power. He sought success through the diffusion of intelligence, the enlightenment of the masses."

The granite sarcophagus near the monument of the elder BENEDICT, to the memory of Brevet Brigadier-General LEWIS BENEDICT, one of Albany's most famous Generals in our late war, is in the Roman style. The ornaments on the top are symbolical of his profession, and comprise an officer's sword, with a wreath of laurel. A scroll near the point of the sword bears the inscription, "Benedictus qui patitur."

If you wish to know what the younger BENEDICT has done to entitle him to the enduring gratitude and veneration of every lover of his

2*

country, you may read an epitome in stone of his
military history, upon the four sides of his memorial. In so doing you will sympathize with the
captive in Williamsburgh, Libby and Salisbury
prisons, glory in the hero of Port Hudson and
Sabine cross-roads, and mourn the departed brave
of Pleasant Hill.

At a meeting of the Bar of Albany, in May,
1864, Judge John K. Porter thus spoke of the
last charge of General BENEDICT — the incident
that sent him here to rest:

"When, at the historic battle of Pleasant Hill,
the fortunes of the day rested for the time on the
bearing of this chosen brigade of the Nineteenth
Army Corps, every man in his command knew
that, whoever else might fail, LEWIS BENEDICT
would not fail — and that, in the bloodiest crisis
of battle, his pulse would be even, his voice firm,
his vision clear, his judgment poised, and his
heart true. It was only such a man in command
of our left wing who could have held that devoted
band, a living breastwork from which the advan-

cing column of the rebel army more than once recoiled — and who, in the end, could move those ranks, unbroken save by death, to the final charge which bore our banner to victory. In that charge he fell, leaving a record which imparts lustre to his name, and confers honor on the city of his birth."

We will now proceed westwardly from BENE-DICT, on the *Tour*, and skirt the southern bank of the ravine beside us for a bird's eye view of its rugged glories and a glimpse through the trees of the deep-embowered and picturesque *CONSECRA-TION LAKE*, a short distance ahead.

First we pass the small Egyptian marble of E. VAN SCHAICK, and the monuments of COULSON, NESSLE, POHLMAN, HALL, MORGAN, and HAL-LENBECK, and GAYLOR SHELDON.

Almost directly opposite SHELDON, a few feet from the road, we see a lot surrounded by an iron fence, which, although it contains little in the way of artificial adornment, we cannot pass without special notice. It is the lot of Rev. BARTHOL-

OMEW T. WELSH, one of the fathers of this institution — its first president — and a gentleman who will long be remembered in this connection for the enthusiasm exhibited by him upon the question of a Rural Cemetery for Albany, when that question was first agitated.

His early history in the city named, is largely the early history of these enchanting grounds. He it was who first gave the project the stimulus, through a public address, that has carried it to a successful issue. To his cogent arguments, maintaining the rights of the dead to quiet rural sepulture, coupled with the hearty co-operation and continued support of the present presiding officer of the association, who has been its friend throughout, the existence of this paragon of mortuary gardens, is, in a great measure, due. The old gentleman now rests peacefully in the beautiful "City of the Silent," whose interests were formerly his tenderest care

Again we advance, passing the monuments of PHILLIPS and VAN BUREN. In the VAN BUREN lot rests Doctor JOHN VAN BUREN, an eminent physician of Albany. Beyond VAN BUREN, on the opposite side, is FRIEND HUMPHREY'S memorial. This gentleman was one of Albany's most successful business men. Several handsome little headstones, adorned with emblematic flowers, grace the lot.

The symmetrical Doric Column of McCAMMON, is next seen. It is crowned with a draped urn, and a wreath of roses encircles the shaft. In the same lot we notice the durable granite of BRUCE.

Still farther on we observe the monument of OSWALD, and the free-stone of LEMUEL STEELE. Here let us turn towards the Ravine and look down upon *CONSECRATION LAKE* through the openings in the veil of foliage that partially intercepts the view. How romantic a spot it seems. And how delicious to drink in, at this little distance, the melody of its music-breathing fountain as it sings a low alto in the morning chorus of the many-voiced birds. As we will soon have an opportunity for a closer view of the Lake, we will dwell no longer here upon its attractions, but will resume our trip past JAMES CLARK, and on to the monument of HARMANUS BLEECKER.

Mr. BLEECKER was a decendant of the celebrated JANS JANSEN BLEECKER, the ancestor of all who bear that name in this State. He was known throughout the State as an eminent advocate, and his name is frequently to be found on the pages of the reports of the days when Kent and Spencer, and Thompson and Van Ness, were the great luminaries of the law. He was a successful politician, and once officiated as Minister to the Hague.

Leaving BLEECKER, we proceed past the STRONG brown stone, and stop before the handsome monument, purely Gothic, of SCHOOLCRAFT and JOHNSON. JOHN L. SCHOOLCRAFT, who once figured largely in public life, lies here.

Beyond SCHOOLCRAFT is a very singular looking rustic cross, commemorative of JOHN INNES KANE and MARY, his wife, the former of whom died at Palermo, Sicily.

Leaving this unique little specimen, we pass

WHITLOCK, and on the opposite side we see a small marble monument to the Rev. DAVID DYER, who died recently. Mr. DYER was for a long time chaplain of the Albany Penitentiary, and was the author of an interesting history of that institution.

As we advance we see the names of POMFRET, E. PERRY and TABER. Here the *TOUR* winds round TABER and leaps the Ravine by means of Glen Cross Bridge. As we do not wish to follow it farther at present, we will continue straight ahead, entering *GLEN CROSS WAY*, which meets us here.

Ascending this slope by the curving road last mentioned, we pass ALEXANDER, and at the abrupt turn beyond we notice the cottage monuments of H. NEWMAN and HUGH HUMPHREY.

The singular Egyptian column of REUEL CLAPP next strikes the eye. Opposite, on our left, a little distance from the road, we see the small monument of MCMULLEN and the cross-crowned memorial of ALLEN. In front of this is another small monument in the lot of L. D. COLLINS. Upon the side towards us appears a harp with one broken string, signifying that a member of a family has departed. Again, in front of COLLINS, stand the memorials of HOWES and MONTEATH.

Here we turn westerly into another portion of the *TOUR* around CLAPP, leaving on our left the small monument of PAYN—a name that sounds familiar to numerous tobacco lovers.

A very odd looking monument here attracts us. It is the large granite globe of PRENTICE, which is emblematic of eternity. This is certainly novel and substantial, if nothing more. Many different opinions are expressed as to its appropriateness and general merits; and the "eternal fitness" question is frequently discussed in consequence. It has these advantages over the majority of monuments: it cannot topple over and is always plumb. Although plain, and, we might say, unpretending, it attracts its share of attention.

Again advancing, we observe the small monument of FRELEIGH and SNYDER, and opposite stands the neat Latin cross of Rev. Dr. POHLMAN. In the same lot is a soldier's rustic memorial, of strange design, to the memory of Lieut. WM. H. POHLMAN, another gallant young Albanian who fell in the late war. You will infer from the many names of memorable battle grounds inscribed upon the stone, that, for a young man of twenty-two, he had considerable experience in war before receiving the wounds that terminated fatally, at Gettysburg, in 1863. His military record stamps him as an energetic and courageous young patriot, while his bouyant spirits, genial disposition, and educational accomplishments, rendered him a most desirable visitor to the social circle.

From POHLMAN, we pass the monuments of ANDREWS, MUIR, SANFORD, ROBINSON and COOK, TELLER, TURNER and VAN ETTEN. We will now again leave the *TOUR*, because in its sudden turn here to the north, around by the WING vault, it departs from our intended line of march.

As we stand here we see to the left, a few steps ahead, the small marble monument of DAVID ROSE. We will turn around it southerly into *PROSPECT AVENUE*. Opposite ROSE, upon a neat

iron enclosure, we read the names of HADLEY and
SEDAN. Then comes the low monument of CHASE,
and beyond, but not facing this avenue, stand the
marble obelisk and sarcophagus of DeForest.

A few steps farther on this avenue is intersected
by *FOREST AVENUE*. In front of us at this point
is a marble monument, surmounted by that frequently recurring emblem of innocence, the dove.
The name of GREER, which it bears, will suggest
pleasant memories to those who indulge in the
Indian weed.

We will cross over to GREER and wind around
it. Standing all alone on the margin of the *DELL*
(*COLD SPRING DELL*) before us, we see the marble monument which commemorates Gen. GEORGE
TALCOTT, Lieut. Col. GEORGE H. TALCOTT, and
their wives.

Let us now descend easterly to the Stone Bridge.
On our left is the marble obelisk of D. MOUNT,
and back of this the elegant headstones of WM.
GODSON.

Farther east is the superb memorial of SOUTH-

WICK, and still farther in the same line is LYMAN
ROOT's large granite monument. The shaft itself
of this is the heaviest on the grounds; but the
monument entire, in consequence of its lacking
the usual massive die, is less in weight than any
one of several others here.

As *PROSPECT AVENUE* crosses the *DELL*, by
means of the Stone Bridge, it suddenly turns to
the west; and if you are agreeable we will humor
its twisting whims a little longer, and turn with it.
But first notice the large granite monument and
splendid circular lot of BENEDICT, on the corner
to the left.

Moving along the south side of the *DELL*, westerly, we see to the left the marble of McCLASKY,
and soon reach the well kept lot of DICKSON, with
its neat enclosure.

We are now upon that part of the *SOUTH RIDGE*
where circular lots are a very prominent and feli-
citous feature. We will be favorably impressed
with this, and will feel a sense of relief in contem-
plating the change from sharp cornered parallelo-

grams, triangles and irregular plats, to the easy
unbroken curve and graceful outline of a circle or
an ellipse. We will notice, too, that uncouth iron
fences — a style of enclosure that detracts much
from the natural rural appearance of any cemetery
where it predominates — and high, impenetrable
hedges, are not in favor on this portion of the
grounds. This will surely meet our unqualified
approbation.

Proceeding up the slope beyond DICKSON, we
see that this avenue takes another devious notion
and darts off southerly, almost at right angles with
its previous course.

We will go straight ahead into *WILD FLOWER
AVENUE ;* but if *you* see fit to keep company still
with the rambling road before mentioned, we will
meet you a little farther on.

Let us tell you what is to be seen on the continuation of *Prospect Avenue.* In farther pursuing it you
will first pass the circular lot of ARCHIBALD McCLURE,
on the right hand corner. Then you will see the handsomely draped soldier's monument to Lieutentant-
Colonel FREDERICK L. TREMAINE, the son of Hon.
Lyman Tremaine.

Young TREMAINE was a heroic soldier, who nobly emulated the example of his Revolutionary ancestors by entering our army during the late war. His military record is the record of gallantry and patriotism. He is commemorated in verse, by Alfred B. Street:

> * * * * "The saddle was his throne, and he a king
>   When the fierce squadron dashed, in thundering might,
> A cataract of swords and shots — a wing
>   Of rushing Havoc — a quick cleaving flight
> Of deadly levin! Lo; a glorious raid!
>   And the galloping steeds and the rush and the clang
> Of the ride over mountain, through forest and glade,
>   And the keen thrilling peals of the trumpet! How sprang
> The hamlet in terror, while on came the burst
> Of the troopers and cheering and flame told the worst,
> As they swept up the harvest and dashed down the wall,
> And laden with spoil skipped away one and all,
> While the night rang with clash and deep thunder of bound,
> And flushed wide with torch-flame, and day heard the sound
> From field and from village, of wailing and wrath,
> And the foe sought in vain to block Sheridan's path.
> And with them our eager young hero! no toil
> Too great for his striving ; no battle turmoil
> Too fierce for his daring; no duty undone
> Till the goal of the striving and daring was won."

Opposite TREMAINE you will see HUNTINGTON'S granite, and next comes the elegant light-colored obelisk of NORTHROP. Its material is the New Hampshire granite.

A little distance farther on you see the VAN VECHTEN granite monument, with Latin cross — a graceful and substantial structure. Here lie ABRAHAM and TEUNIS VAN VECHTEN, two distinguished Albany lawyers.

At a certain period in the past, when Albany was the recognized legal centre of the State, ABRAHAM VAN VECHTEN was one of the brightest stars among the fraternity — one of the most able jurists that ever shed

3*

lustre upon the Bar of Albany. The high places were then filled by a gifted race of advocates, among whom were Hamilton, Harrison, Jones, Burr, and Livingston. But their brilliancy could not cast young VAN VECHTEN in the shade. He ranked among his illustrious seniors as an equal and a competitor for the highest professional eminence. His talents were too conspicuous to allow him to confine his efforts to the Bar. He repeatedly represented his fellow-citizens in the Legislature. At an early period of his life he declined a seat on the bench of the Supreme Court. He has been Recorder of Albany, State Senator, and Attorney-General, and was a member of the Constitutional Convention of 1821. He died at Albany on the 6th of January, 1837.

Next you are attracted by the very substantial granite monument of Hon. HUGH WHITE. He by whom it was erected was recently buried beside it. It is surmounted by a Grecian urn. It is massive without being clumsy, beautiful without being frail; and looks as though it might stand for endless ages to mark the resting place of one of the fathers of that spindle city not far distant, which, with eminent propriety, has recently taken on municipal airs and attributes.

Now you approach the WARD monument, and near it notice several handsome little sculptured headstones.

A little farther on this avenue crosses the *Tour*. Near their intersection are the handsome headstones of WILLIAM MASCRAFT and wife.

You pass the monument of YOUNG and to the south see KELLEY'S granite obelisk.

In proceeding into *WILD FLOWER AVENUE* we pass McCLURE'S circle on the left, and soon see the conspicuous monument of MONTEATH.

Lith of G.W. Lewis 452 Broadway. Albany.

NELSON.

Here the avenue turns southerly and gives us a front view of that structure. Four handsome sculptured headstones, commemorative of different members of the MONTEATH family, attend it.

Opposite MONTEATH stands the very graceful octagonal shaft of S. H. COOK, and some distance south of this the fine monument of JEFFERS. Here is a double headstone, with cross, and bearing one of the several emblems of faith—joined hands.

Again in advancing we see the Egyptian obelisk of NELSON, with Roman moulds and polished tablets. It is eventually intended to commemorate the "Twin Brothers," and one of the twain is already here. It was erected by Doctor ALEXANDER NELSON, of Albany.

The next prominent monument we notice is that to RUFUS KING. Its material is Quincy granite, and it stands second in size among the monumental structures of the place. Mr. KING, who died but recently, was one of the most successful and respected self-made men of Albany.

To the right, beyond the *Tour*, which meets us here, we see two superior specimens of the sculptor's art. One is Palmer's great masterpiece, the "Angel at the Sepulchre." The other is the elaborate memorial of JAMES A. WILSON.

As this last is the nearer of the two, we will cross the *Tour* and contemplate from in front its artistic beauties. It is one of the most costly monuments on the ground, and will bear the closest inspection. A niche in the front contains a faultless figure of Faith. Survey the monument carefully and observe the richness of its tracery. The handsome lot upon which it stands could not possibly be more appropriately adorned, and the memorial is destined to attract much attention. The celebrated Launitz, of New York, is the author of this exquisite production. It was erected in the year 1870, by Mrs. JAMES A. WILSON, to the memory of her husband, who was formerly a prominent Albany merchant.

Southerly from WILSON we see the immense plat of ERASTUS CORNING, which is the largest in the Cemetery, and has cost a moderate fortune. A monumental granite cross, to the memory of GERTRUDE TIBBITTS CORNING, is, as yet, its only memorial; but we understand that here is destined to be reared the most stately monument in the Cemetery, and one of the largest in the country. Fancy a colossal monument of—we will say—one hundred feet in height, upon the elevated summit of *PROSPECT HILL*, and tell us would it not be an imposing structure?

We are now standing on the east side of the CORNING plat; and our commanding position affords us a most charming view of the surrounding country. To the northeast appears the city of Troy, pulsing with the excitement of its tumultuous thousands, and sending upwards, in fantastic disorder, its myriad hazy columns from the sentinel-like chimnies of countless manufactories. Beyond are the ambitious mountains piling up to the clouds, and seeming, as they recede, to lose themselves in the embrace of the distant horizon. Nearer, we trace the course of the sinuous Hudson downward from the bustling city for several miles, until at last, with a sudden turn, it "silently steals away" behind the wooded islands to the south.

But let us leave these foreign attractions and turn our attention once more to the native beauties of this "Silent City." We will walk around the CORNING plat and gaze upon the memorial of an old Revolutionary hero.

Here we find a splendid Roman column to the memory of General PHILIP SCHUYLER, who lies beneath. The lot was recently dedicated to this purpose by the Trustees of the Cemetery, and the monument was erected by Mrs. W. STARR MILLER, a lineal descendant of the General. The name of SCHUYLER is intimately connected with the early history of Albany, and stands conspicuous in our Colonial annals. One of the ancestors of the General was mayor of Albany and commander of the northern militia as far back as 1690. The General was born in Albany in 1733, and at an early age he began to display his active mind and military spirit. He was a captain in the New York levies at Fort Edward, in 1775, and accompanied the British army in the expedition down lake George in the summer of 1758. He was with Lord Howe when he fell 'by the fire of the enemy on landing at the north end of the lake; and he was appointed to convey the body of that young and lamented nobleman to Albany, where he was buried, with appropriate ceremonies, in the Episcopal church. He was present at the capture of Burgoyne, and was highly complimented by that General for his urbanity of manner and chivalric magnanimity. A daughter of General SCHUYLER was married to the brilliant Alexander Hamilton, the victim of the unfortunate Hamilton-Burr duel.

The General was first interred in the VAN RENS-SELAER vault at Albany, and afterwards removed to a vault on these grounds, where he lay without a monument to mark his place of sepulture. That fact having recently been laid before the Trustees of the Cemetery, and also the fact that Mrs. W. STARR MILLER desired to erect to him a fitting

memorial, it was decided by them to select a plat
in a prominent location, wherein to

> " Gather him to his grave again
> And solemnly and softly lay,
> Beneath the verdure of the plain,
> The warrior's scattered bones away."

The preamble to the resolutions presented by
Judge Harris before the annual meeting, at which
official action was taken upon the matter, contains
the following:

"In the dim galleries of the past, where now
hang the portraits which commemorate the good,
the gifted, and the brave, who 'pledged their lives,
their fortunes, and their honor' to the cause of
liberty in the stormiest days of the Revolution, no
one more deservedly challenges admiration than
does that of him who only asks of us a grave.
Among all those grand actors in the heroic history
of our country, whose shadowy outlines are now
but faintly visible through the smoke of revolution and the haze of an intervening century,
surely none should be more proudly recognized
by the citizens of Albany than General PHILIP

SCHUYLER. * * * * It is eminently fitting that this beautiful city of the dead, so near to the home where he dwelt while living, and where slumber the descendants of friends and neighbors who stood, perchance with him, shoulder to shoulder in the contest of the past, should furnish for his remains a resting place."

Then followed resolutions, which were adopted, and the result of which confronts us here.

Now let us proceed round by the west side of CORNING to the famous "Angel at the Sepulchre." It adorns the lot of ROBERT LENNOX BANKS. Read the scriptural passage in which the artist found his inspiration, and judge for yourself of the success which has attended his efforts to embody the idea in stone:

"And behold there was a great earthquake; for the angel of the Lord descended from heaven, and came and rolled back the stone from the door and sat upon it. His countenance was like lightning and his raiment white as snow, and for fear of him the keepers did quake and become as dead men."

The following description of the "Angel" in embryo, is from the pen of a competent art critic:

"Being of the favored few who saw this in the clay, time can never efface the impressions produced by that first view, while it was yet in an early stage of progress. Towards evening we went into the studio with the sculptor, who carried a lighted candle, and as we entered we saw before and above us, in the dim uncertain light, an imperfectly defined form of angelic strength and loveliness, which seemed gazing, with unlimited vision, far away into infinity, and behind it darkness and shadow, as of the unknown tomb. As we stood awe-struck and speechless, the statute seemed to live, the breast to heave, the face to be distinct with heavenly intelligence, and we waited, fairly expecting from the lips the imperishable inquiry, 'Why seek ye the living among the dead?'"

As we turn from the peerless creation before us — a subject which, in the future, we will surely find an ever new delight — and look westwardly, we observe on our right, a short distance below, a

pretty pear-shaped lakelet, surrounding a minia-
ture island, luxuriantly clad in nature's green.

Its eminent adaptedness to the location would
seem to indicate that it was one of the original
contributions to the beauty of these highly favored
grounds, with which the place has been so profusely blessed by the great Architect.

There are other lakes here, wild and romantic,
with the mark of Nature's handiwork still fresh
upon them, that were evidently "born, not made."
In this case, however, Nature simply pointed out
the spot and left Art to improve upon the sug-
gestion.

The construction and embellishment of the
highly ornamental " *CYPRESS WATER*," was accom-
plished at the cost of considerable labor and
expense. It was commenced in November, 1869,
and finished in the short time of one month, under
the direction of Superintendent THOMAS.

You will perceive how admirably it harmo-
nizes with the native conformation of the con-
tiguous ground. Commencing at the head of

COLD SPRING DELL, its graceful curves gradually diverge until finally its covers, with its aqueous contents, a space that a short time ago was entirely occupied by a disagreeable, unsightly, bog-hole.

A number of springs, issuing from under the little island in the centre, constitute its chief, though not its only source of supply. The copious stream flowing through the Ravine, which separates the *SOUTH* and *MIDDLE RIDGES,* has, through the medium of a hydraulic ram, and a quarter of a mile of pipe, been made to do service as an auxiliary; and fully provides against any scarcity of water that might arise from a lack of sufficiency in its natural feeders.

The most gratifying feature of this improvement is the effect which it has had in enhancing the value of the lots in its vicinity. Ground which, a short time ago, was perfectly unsalable on any terms, is now eagerly sought after at prices ranging from one hundred to two hundred and fifty dollars for each lot of two hundred and fifty-six superficial feet. A useless swamp has given

Lith of G. W. Lewis 452 Broadway, Albany.

BRUMAGHIM.

way to several sections of dry, eligible burial sites, which have been laboriously and patiently graded up and put in order for sale.

We will descend towards the lake, leaving SHERWOOD and CONKLIN on the right. About half way down the slope we see the handsome lot of BRUMAGHIM and its adornments, of which our manual presents a partial illustration. The two memorials which it contains, though small, are decidedly attractive. That principal headstone, with its delicate drapery, was evidently executed by an artist. As the declining sun irradiates the translucent marble of which this little gem is composed, the effect is peculiar and striking. You will notice its attendant memorial, which represents a tree trunk, entwined in ivy, upon which perches a dove.

Now we see the monument of SALISBURY, the neat lot of BENDER, and a broken column to Col. HOWARD CARROLL, a distinguished officer in our late war, who was highly esteemed for his bravery and devotion to the cause.

Next we perceive the tastefully arranged circular

4*

lot of DAWSON. Here is a soldier's monument upon which we read the name of Maj. GEORGE S. DAWSON; a young patriot than whom no victim of the rebellion was more deeply mourned by friends and fellow soldiers. He particularly distinguished himself in the battles of the Wilderness, and his military record is made the subject of a poem by Albany's celebrated bard.

" All through the crimsoned wilderness he went,
  With strength untiring and with soul unbent,
  All through, all through, the same young brave, the
    same!
  Through the fierce hurricane of blood and flame! "

We have now reached " *CYPRESS WATER*," which has just been spoken of at length, and will cross to the opposite side of *COLD SPRING DELL*. If we should take the first turn beyond to the right into *ROSELEAF AVENUE*, thence into a portion of the *TOUR*, thence into *PINE BOUGH AVENUE*, we would find much to engross our attention. But as our route leads us in a different direction, we will simply tell you what may be seen by taking the trip mentioned.

First on the right of *Roseleaf Avenue* is the ANDER-
SON monument. Then the soldier's monument to Lieut.
JAMES WILLIAMSON, another martyr to the rebellion.
Back of this is a neat brown-stone to JOHN WILLIAMS,
and a handsome marble obelisk to JOHN FAIRBURN.
Opposite, next ahead, is ROSSMAN'S low, durable gran-
ite, with large urn.

. Then you see two fine circular lots on opposite sides
of the avenue, that on the right belonging to STEPHEN
MUNSON, a gentleman widely known in the shoe and
leather market.

Winding to the right around MUNSON into a part of
the *Tour*, the lot of S. CUNLIFF is seen. A little farther on is the large granite to General RICE, the hero
of twenty hard fought battles. Its incriptions will
interest you. Not one of Albany's patriots has left a
more glorious record than the Christian soldier to whom
this memorial is dedicated. From a private he rapidly
rose, strictly upon his merits, to the rank of Brigadier-
General. After passing through many sanguinary
engagements, his twentieth battle brought with it the
fatal ball. He was wounded in the thigh, and lived but
two hours after undergoing the tortures of amputation.
Mr. J. G. Holland thus poetically alludes to his last
coherent expression, which is among the inscriptions
upon his monument :

" ' TURN ME,' he said, ' THAT I MAY DIE
    FACE TO THE FOE !' and ready hands
And loyal hearts were waiting by
    To execute his last commands.

" Facing the enemy he died
    A hero in his latest breath,
And now with mingled love and pride
    I weep and boast his glorious death.

"No braver words than these, my friend,
Have ever sealed a soldier's tongue;
No nobler words hath history penned;
No finer words hath poet sung."

Opposite RICE is ROSELLE's attractive granite. Soon you see the elegant monumental tribute, from his congregation, to Rev. J. N. CAMPBELL. One of the inscriptions reads as follows:

"As a preacher, he was pungent, logical, eloquent. As a minister of Christ, faithful unto death."

Now you pass the STEELE monument, and a little further on turn abruptly round the tall plain marble column of RIDDER, on left westerly into *Forest Avenue*. The Scotch granite of VAN DYCK, with its intense, mirror-like polish, is on your right. No other material combines more happily the elements of durability and beauty.

You advance past J. R. COLEMAN, H. J. COULDWELL and I. N. KEELER. Here is the monument of JOHN E. PAGE. In this lot is a pretty little morsel of sculpture inscribed to "Our dear little ELLA."

THOMPSON's marble tree—emblem of an unfinished life—appears, then the monument of D. W. LAWYER, and the lofty granite shaft of THOMAS McCREDIE. In this last are durability, beauty, and charming simplicity harmoniously blended. The monument is entirely plain, if we except the emblematic thistle which graces the shaft.

Opposite and ahead is W. P. IRWIN's tall marble, around which you may turn into another part of *Rose-leaf Avenue*. Moving westerly you see the brown stone, with urn, of JOHN ZEH, and on the next corner ahead, at the *Tour*, is the PARKE monument.

Here turn northerly into the *Tour*, and notice the

Lith of G.W.Lewis 452 Broadway. Albany.

WOOSTER.

marble of ABSALOM ANDERSON, the monument of JOHN STACKPOLE, and that of GUNSALUS and PERRIGO. The names of TURNBULL, COOPER and KINNEY, will then be seen.

Leaving *CYPRESS WATER* behind, we proceed on the *TOUR*, past *ROSELEAF AVENUE*, to the next right hand turn which we take around TEN EYCK. Several neat lots are passed, and then our path is intercepted by another portion of the *TOUR*. A marble monument on the right hand corner, at the junction, bears the name of JACOB SLACK.

We turn to the left, northerly, and read the names of QUINN, WOOD and AIKEN. Before us is WOOSTER'S imposing figure of Hope, a production which we will study with more than ordinary pleasure. The figure stands upon an octagonal pedestal, richly wrought in emblematic vines and flowers. It commands universal admiration.

Southwest of WOOSTER, and facing that portion of the *TOUR* which we have recently left, is the very touching little memorial of STICKNEY. Although it is off our route, we will take this short cross road to the left and reach it. It is a monumental headstone, with a niche in front containing the standing figure of a child. Upon a scroll above, interlaced with a garland of flowers, the simple inscription "IDA" appears. Those three solitary letters speak more forcibly to the heart, and are more suggestive of real grief and never-dying love than the most fulsome epitaph. But we will return to WOOSTER.

The western terminus of *EVERGREEN PATH*, a most enchanting walk, is on our right. Before resuming our course northerly from WOOSTER'S figure, we will tell you what may be seen upon the path named.

As you enter, the charming vista directs your eye through its gradually narrowing lines, which seem in the distance to complete their convergence and shut out all beyond. The first monument seen is that of GROES-BECK, and then the names of BEEBE, McMILLAN, FORD, COX and BOYLE are read.

The next attraction is the large rustic granite cross to Col. GEORGE W. PRATT, who was a gallant soldier, a distinguished linguist, and a young man of great ability and promise.

Cross an intersecting road and you will observe a pretty little piece of sculpture, to "EMMA," on the lot of

Wm. N. Strong. The handsome monument of Smith is seen, and then the memorials of Noyes, John Kennedy, Osborne, Johnston and Becker. In going further on in this path you will see nothing more of importance but what our general route will bring to your notice.

Leaving Wooster on the left, we continue northerly in the *Tour*, past the octagonal shaft of John Moore, and then read the names of Winne, Gladding and P. P. Staats. The monuments of John Ellery, J. A. Buckbee and John L. Staats are passed.

Now come four hedge-enclosed lots, the last of which is adorned by the granite monument of George I. Amsdell. Next is the solid marble of T. M. Amsdell. As we follow on, the *Tour* takes an easterly sweep, and moving by the lots of Stevens and Elmendorf, and John S. Dickerman—a name well known to many who have been obliged to commit their worldly effects to the tender mercies of the highest bidder—we turn sharply to the right into *Lawn Avenue*.

Our course now, for a short distance, is southerly. First, on our right, is Feltman's marble;

and the names of COWELL, LANSING and JAMES
D. JONES appear before we reach the large oblong
plat of A. S. CLARK, J. AUSTIN and J. J. AUSTIN.
Beyond this is MERRIFIELD's monument, and
back of the latter stands CHESTER PACKARD's tall
marble. In the PACKARD lot is a winged figure.

We continue past C. A. JONES, D. A. SMITH, P.
W. HOLMES and C. H. WINNE. KNOWLTON and
CARY are on our right.

Soon *LAWN AVENUE* winds easterly and brings
us back of *HIGHLAND WATER*, a circular lakelet,
which, like *CYPRESS WATER*, is thickly populated
with different families of the finny tribe. The
gold fish seem to be the lords of the colony. If
you are interested in the study of ichthyology you
will enjoy a call upon the glistening nobility of
this little aquarium. You may pass between the
intervening lots, and by means of the steps which
descend to it, find footing on a level with the
water. If none of the inhabitants are immediately
visible, a pebble thrown upon the bosom of the
pond, near you, will cause them to promptly rise

and swarm to your feet. Now take a crumb of
almost anything that is eatable, hold it near the
surface of the water, and see how long it will re-
main before some veteran golden-coated epicure
will dart forward and unceremoniously snap from
your fingers the coveted morsel. If your first
advances should fail to induce the piscatorial
familiarity intimated, you will please not accuse
us of insinuating a "fish story," for really these
little gourmands are remarkably tame. Probably
the habit so extensively indulged in by visitors, of
feeding them with titbits brought along for the
occasion, explains the phenomenon.

Now if you have said good bye to our aquatic
friends, and returned to *LAWN AVENUE*, we will
again move easterly. To the right is a small un-
attractive monument to SAMUEL SAGUE. "Sam.,"
as he was popularly called, was an oracle among
horsemen, a wit of the first water, and a person as
extensively known, perhaps, in his day, as any
similar character.

As we progress, the gothic monument of EDSON,

with its sarcophagus, appears on our left. Opposite, and almost hidden by tall evergreens, is the lot in which are entombed the heads of four generations of the famous Albany house of VAN RENSSELAER. It is possible, although not certain, that this lot also contains the remains of KILLIAN VAN RENS-SELAER, the original patroon, whose record, as you are well aware, forms an important and interesting part of our colonial history. Hon. D. D. Barnard, in a discourse upon STEPHEN VAN RENSSELAER (one of the four STEPHENS to whom we have before alluded as being buried here), who died in 1839, says of KILLIAN:

"The power of the patroon of that day was analogous to that of the old feudal barons — acknowledging the government of New Amsterdam and States General as his superiors. He had his own fortress, planted with his own cannon, manned with his own soldiers, with his own flag waving over them. The courts of the colony were his own courts, where the gravest questions and the highest crimes were cognizable; but with

appeal in the more important cases. Justice was administered in his own name. The colonists were his immediate subjects, and took the oath of fealty and allegiance to him."

Our next advance brings in view the plain, attractive lot of SAMUEL H. RANSOM. The large obelisk of Quincy granite which adorns it, is by many considered the best proportioned monument in the Cemetery.

We continue on past ESMAY, VAN LOON and WOOLVERTON, and soon come to the junction of three roads. Before us is the brown-stone of WM. SHEPPARD, and opposite, on our right, is the marble monument of B. C. BRAINARD. That narrow road in front of BRAINARD, which leads north-easterly around SHEPPARD, will bring us into *ROSELAND WAY.* We will take it, and see the monument of J. H. TEN EYCK; and opposite this a very striking little structure of polished Scotch granite, surmounted by a chaste marble figure. It is the memorial of ROBINSON and HOWE, and is one of the most delightful little specimens we have

yet seen. The great admiration it receives is partly
due to the fact that it embodies that highly appropriate idea for a cemetery memorial — Remembrance. The darker color of the polished pedestal
gives pleasing prominence to the pure white marble figure, so sweet in expression, graceful in form
and pose, and perfect in finish.

Immediately back of ROBINSON and HOWE, near
the small HENDRICKSON marble, lies HENRY T.
MEECH. "HARRY" MEECH was well known in
Albany as the popular proprietor and manager of
the old Museum, during the prosperous days of
that institution.

In front of ROBINSON is WINNE'S free-stone, and
the marble structure of JAMES MORROW can be
seen to the right. We wind around WINNE, and
observe a venerable brown-stone, which, through
its weather-beaten appearance, speaks of many
years' service. Among other names, it preserves
that of Col. HENRY QUACKENBUSH, who "was
with Lord Amherst at Ticonderoga, with General
Gates at Saratoga, in the days that tried men's

souls." We also glean from the stone that " his servant and faithful slave, " NANCY," is buried here.

The *Tour* is met once more. If we look westerly from the junction we will see, not far away, a fine substantial marble mausoleum. It belongs to the SEYMOUR family. We purpose proceeding towards it, but not before at least speaking to you of certain attractive objects located east from QUACKENBUSH, to our right on the *Tour*, and also on the first converging road beyond. The little trip alluded to cannot be conveniently made in a carriage, because the turn from the *Tour* into the road last mentioned is too sharp to admit of a connexion by that means.

The first object that arrests the eye east of QUACK-ENBUSH is a most faithful imitation of a tree trunk, in brown-stone. It was erected by Dr. ARMSBY. The appropriate color of the material, the climbing vines behind, and the green moss clinging to the front, combine to give it a wonderful resemblance to the lower portion of a living tree.

Opposite ARMSBY is the granite of L. SPRAUGE PARSONS, and next is STIMSON's neat memorial. On the right is McINTYRE's marble sarcophagus. This is one of the many superior specimens which have come from the hands of Launitz, of New York. In the same lot is HENDERSON's figure. DUNLOP's brown-stone is ahead, and then comes the monument to JOHN I. WENDELL, who for several years was an active and efficient member of the Albany Cemetery Association, and one of the most devoted friends of the institution represented by that body. The sentiments of the board towards a departed brother are fittingly perpetuated in an inscription upon the stone. Dr. PETER WENDELL, who in the early part of the present century was one of Albany's most distinguished physicians, occupies a place in the same lot.

This locality is called *Roseland Hill*. Here is another lovely view of *Consecration Lake*. *Ravine Crossway* opens on the left. Upon it are some fine monuments. There is the brown-stone of REED and SPELLMAN, the granite of CYRUS HAWLEY, and beyond the names of DAVIS and WILKINSON may be seen. The circular lot of B. P. LEARNED, with its octagonal shaft of granite, is farther on, and still ahead the names of WM. McELROY, RUFUS W. PECKHAM and FORSYTH appear.

Now from *ROSELAND WAY* we turn towards SEYMOUR's structure, winding around POWERS on our left. Passing WM. NEWTON, the monument of D. LATHROP is observed, and here is the mausoleum — a very creditable piece of architecture — which we have before noticed at a distance. This short cross road to the left is called *OAK FOREST WAY*. Proceeding in this we see NEWTON's granite, and after crossing another portion of the *TOUR*, past the free-stone of ADAMS and HUN, and the marble of SANFORD, we meet *GREENWOOD AVE-NUE*, which we turn into northwesterly. The lot of TILLINGHAST is observed, and also that one, neatly coped, of DEY ERMAND and SPELLMAN. Opposite this last is the broken column — an emblem which, perhaps, you will think too frequently repeated on these grounds — to ALEXAN-DER CAMPBELL, and beside it a marble obelisk to DANIEL CAMPBELL, erected by the young men of Albany. On this side of the latter an inscription preserves an enduring record of the deed, while a figure of Grief occupies a niche on the reverse.

Next comes GOODWIN's low granite, and opposite is the memorial of ADAM TODD. We move along by ROBINSON's free-stone, and the lot of ALFRED MOSHER. Here is VAN ANTWERP's winged figure. It is a fine piece of sculpture, and one which demands more than a transient glance. We might look upon it as the guardian angel of the locality.

Keeping on, we see DENNISON's monument, and the pretty Gothic marble of EDWARD OWENS. Here is CRUTTENDEN's cross, and now we pause for a moment before the KING monuments. That soldier's memorial is to ROBERT H. KING; and those devices upon its face are intended to represent certain testimonials presented to him during the late war, by our Navy Department, as a recognition of his gallant conduct and patriotic services. Upon the other side is VAN DER WERKEN's small marble, and ahead are the monuments of TOWNSEND, McELROY and MARTIN. The obelisk of GEORGE F. GRAY is seen, and then, on the left, a lot containing a marble monument and enclosed by a curving iron fence. This is WILLIAM J. WALKER's.

Here is the *TOUR* again. We will turn round WALKER and advance in it southerly. The lot of CRAPO is passed, and the monuments of JOHN FEATHERLY and FRISBY. A headstone here commemorates the brave Col. EDWARD FRISBY, who was killed near Crentreville, Va., while leading his regiment to assault.

Not far ahead is the brown-stone to Captain
THOMAS BAYEUX—a tribute from the Albany
Burgess Corps. Directly east of this is a novel
rustic monument to the brothers JAMES L. and
JOHN M. DEMPSEY, the one of whom received fatal
wounds at the battle of Cedar Creek, the other in
an assault on Fort Fisher before Petersburg.

We next see the MIX lot and its five superb
headstones. On again, past JAMES MIX, LONG and
SILSBY, BISHOP, GOWER, COOK, WINTERS, CHASE,
CUSHMAN, BURHANS, and we are before GILES W.
PORTER's very odd looking structure. To our right
is *HIGHLAND WATER*, which we have previously
seen from the other side, and opposite is the marble
cottage monument of BULLION. One of a number of modest headstones here commemorates
"Father;" and Reverend PETER BULLION lies
beneath. By how many thousands is that name
associated with vivid recollections of weary hours
and days spent in endeavoring to elucidate gram-
matical conundrums. Fifteen years ago, BULLION's
grammar was almost an indispensable instrument

in the hands of those who essayed to develop the young idea. Although it has since lost something of its popularity, it still holds an honored place among the text books of the period.

Next to BULLION is WEED'S marble monument. Many ridiculous notions have prevailed concerning the meaning of the figure by which it is surmounted. It is intended to illustrate some Scriptural idea; but what that idea is, we have been unable to discover. The memorial is very neat and appropriate.

Still on in the *Tour* we observe the names of COBB, HAMILTON, MARTIN, VISSCHER and WILSON. Then a large irregular lot, dotted with brown-stone monuments of all shapes and sizes, is noticed on our left. This is the JAMES lot. A new structure, in keeping with its neighbors, bears the name of Rev. WILLIAM JAMES, an eminent divine who died recently.

Opposite the JAMES lot, on our right, lies Dr. WILLIAM BAY, who, at the time of his death, was one of the oldest—if not the oldest—of the medical fraternity in Albany. Dr. BAY was one of the most distinguished of that school of physicians who won "golden opinions" in this vicinity in the early part of the present century.

We are now in *OAKWOOD FOREST*. Leaving JAMES and passing a few small monuments on our right and an oblong plat surrounded by an iron fence, we find that the *TOUR* crosses *GREENWOOD AVENUE*. We turn into the latter round the small marble to the WADDELL family, on our right. On the left is the lot of JOHN J. HILLS. It contains two monuments—one to ISAAC McMURDY and one to SARAH M. CARSON. Years ago, when really fine monuments were rare on these grounds, the drapery of this last was much admired; but the fact that many finer specimens and far greater attractions are now to be found here, has rather tended to cast it in the shade.

On again southerly, in *GREENWOOD AVENUE*, and we see a small brown-stone to the widow of DANIEL STEELE. Opposite is the large irregular plat of KIDD, TEN BROECK and others.

You will realize from the familiar appearance of the objects around us that we were in this vicinity at a previous point in our ramble; but as this is the first instance in which we have brought you twice over the same road, you will probably not complain that the trip has been monotonous.

Let us move easterly around KIDD and, passing the monument of B. C. BRAINERD, which is one of those we have before seen, continue on, by EVERTSON and the splendid granite obelisk of MITCHELL and CUNNINGHAM, to the low brown-stone in the lot of HALL and FRY.

Now we see, at some distance to the left, and standing on the *Tour* beyond, the brown-stone vault of WING. We will take this sharp turn northerly, and, pausing before the WING vault, notice opposite the marble of ROGERS. Directly behind this is BRITTON'S urn-crowned memorial. Near by the latter is the vault of NARCISSE REMOND. The monument of Rev. ISAAC N. WYCKOFF is left behind, and as we descend, following the easterly sweep of the *Tour*, the names of JAMES WILSON, SIDNEY GUEST, and DONCASTER appear.

We are leaving the southern division of the grounds. Our descent is becoming precipitous; and, as the 'verdant bluff rises abruptly to right and left and the densely wooded hills grow rapidly over us, our sense of seclusion—that feeling ever sweet to the meditative mind—is agreeably intensified with every step. We are on one of those sequestered roads which contribute so much to the attractiveness of this " garden of graves," and of which, with fast increasing pleasure, we will see more, as we progress. Although so far, much of art has come under our observation—and something too, perhaps, of human vanity—yet the most fascinating manifestations of nature, in her loveliest garb, are still in prospective. But we will anticipate no farther.

Still descending, we pass under Glen Cross Bridge, and, diving down yet deeper between the hills, we finally reach the terminus of the glade

6

only to feast our eyes upon the romantic scenery of the deep-set, placid *CONSECRATION LAKE.*

It would seem as if this grand natural amphi-theatre might have been foreordained the scene of those solemn ceremonies which dedicated these grounds to the many dead. It *was* that scene at least; and here, while the flashing fountain—

> " Like sheet lightning
> Ever brightening
> With a low melodious thunder "

whispers its hospitable greeting, we will avail our-selves of the ample accommodations for repose which the place affords the visitor, and beguile our half hour's rest by looking back upon the most memorable event in the history of the Rural Cemetery.

The following extracts are taken from a report of the consecration ceremonial, which appeared in the Albany Argus, of Oct. 8th, 1844. This report was published many years ago in pamphlet form, but the little work is now probably out of exist-ence. If you have never before read the beautiful

CONSEGF

Lith of G.W.Lewis 452 Broadway Albany.

IRON LANE

hymn of Miss Woodbridge, or the admirable dedicatory poem of Alfred B. Street, which constituted a part of its contents, you will, no doubt, think with us that these waifs, at least, are well worth the saving:

"The ceremonial of the consecration of the grounds selected by the Albany Cemetery Association, for a general place of burial, took place yesterday, agreeably to the published arrangements. The civic and religious ceremonies were all appropriate, impressive, happily conceived and most happily carried out by the gentlemen to whose hands the duty was confided, and were in admirable adaptation to an occasion, which will be memorable in the history of our ancient but steadily advancing metropolis.

"The very great concourse of citizens who visited the grounds on the occasion—the large number of ladies—the general turnout of military companies, firemen and civic associations—were in themselves encouraging indications of the general interest felt in the success of this important undertaking—

and, we are sure, may be regarded as an earnest of a determination among all sects and classes of our citizens to unite cordially in carrying out to a successful issue, one of the greatest public enterprises of which our city can boast.

"The duties of Marshal were well discharged by General Rufus King, assisted by several gentlemen. The Rev. Dr. Welch and T. W. Olcott, Esq., were the efficient committee of arrangement.

"The place selected and prepared for the ceremonial, was in one of those secluded and beautiful spots with which the location abounds—being a level but irregular space of about half an acre, enclosed on the south by an abrupt and thinly-wooded hill. On the north, hills of a less elevation enclosed the area, and nearly through the centre runs a clear stream of water, which even at this season of the year, holds on its course, and is indeed perennial. Upon this area, were temporary seats, skirting the foot of the hill on the south, and admirably arranged all over it to command a

view of the staging from which the speakers were
to address the multitude.

" Long before the procession reached the ground,
these seats were occupied—hundreds having pre-
ceded the train, and the larger portion of them
ladies, and taken possession. The scene presented,
as the escort came up and opened for the passage
of the procession, was indescribable. The solemn,
dirge-like music—the heavy measured tread and
gay uniform of the military and firemen—the
gorgeous foliage, which at this season distinguishes
our rural scenery—the romantic wildness of the
place itself—and the large concourse assembled—
all conspired to give to the scene an impressive and
sublime character.

" The military, firemen, ladies and citizens having taken the positions assigned them—and nothing
could exceed the order and decorum with which
everything was done—the full and rich harmonies
of one of the best bands to which we ever listened,
gave place to the vocal music from a choir of several hundred singers, who, under the lead of Mr.

6*

R. Packard, sang in full chorus, a Hymn, written by Miss Sarah McDonald, of the Female Academy, to the tune of Rosseau's Dream.

"The Consecrating Prayer, by the Rev. Dr. Sprague, was highly appropriate and impressive, and was listened to with reverent and profound attention.

"The following Hymn, written by Miss A. D. Woodbridge, of the Female Academy, was then sung by the choir:

" This holy ground beneath our feet,
  These gentle sloping hills above,
These silent glades and valleys sweet,
  Shall be the home of those we love.

" Above their couch shall flow'rets bloom—
  Dear, precious flowers, that droop and die,
'Tis fit that ye should wreathe the tomb,
  Where those we best have loved, shall lie.

" But they shall wake when o'er the earth
  Time's last receding wave shall roll;
Shall share in an immortal birth,
  The changeless spring-time of the soul.

" Then let us learn to bear aright
  Life's weary weight of pain and care,
Till, with our heavenly home in sight,
  This last and dreamless couch we share.

"Oh! let us see thy glory here,
  Our Father! and we'll kiss the rod;
We leave ourselves, and all most dear,
  With Thee, our Saviour and our God!

"The Poem, by A. B. Street, Esq. (to whom we are indebted for a copy) was then pronounced, as follows:

"When life's last breath has faintly ebb'd away,
And nought is left but cold unconscious clay,
Still doth Affection bend in anguish deep,
O'er the pale brow to fondly gaze and weep.
What tho' the soul hath soar'd in chainless flight,
Round the spurn'd frame still plays a sacred light,
A hallow'd radiance never to depart,
Pour'd from its solemn source the stricken heart.
Not to the air should then be given the dead,
Not to the flame, nor yet cold ocean's bed,
But to the earth—the earth from whence it rose,
There should the frame be left to its repose.

"There the great Mother guards her holy trust,
Spreads her green mantle o'er the sleeping dust;
There glows the sunshine—there the branches wave,
And birds yield song, flowers fragrance round the
    grave.
There oft to hold communion do we stray,
There droops our mourning memory when away,
And e'en when years have pass'd, our homeward feet
Seek first with eager haste that spot to greet,
And the fond hope lives ever in our breast
When death too claims us, there our dust shall rest.

" All these fair grounds with lavish beauty spread,
  Nature's sweet charms—we give them to the dead;
  Those swelling uplands, whence the raptured sight
  Drinks in the landscape smiling rich and bright,
  Woodlands and meadows, trees and roofs and rills,
  The glittering river, and the fronting hills;
  That nestling dell, with bowery limbs o'erhead,
  And this its brother opening to the tread,
  Each with its naiad tripping low along,
  Striving to hide, but freely offering song;
  Those old deep woods, where Nature wild and
      rude,
  Has built a throne for musing solitude,
  Where sunshine scarce finds way to shrub and
      moss,
  And lies the fractured trunk the earth across,
  These winding paths that lead the wandering feet,
  Through minster-aisles and arbors dim and sweet,
  To soothe thy discord into harmony,
  Oh solemn, solemn death, we dedicate to thee.

" Here will his steps the mourning husband bend,
  With sympathizing Nature for his friend;
  In the low murmur of the pine, he'll hear
  The voice that once was music to his ear;
  In the light waving of the bough, he'll view
  The form that sunshine once around him threw.
  As the reft mother threads each leafy bower,
  Her infant's looks will smile from every flower;
  Its laugh will echo in the warbling glee
  Of every bird that flits from tree to tree;
  In the dead trunk, laid prostrate by the storm,
  The child will see its perish'd parent's form;
  And in the sighing of the evening breath,
  Will hear those faltering tones late hush'd in death.

"Through these branch'd paths will Contemplation
    wind,
And grave wise Nature's teachings on his mind;
As the white grave-stones glimmer to his eye,
A solemn voice will thrill him, "*thou* must die;"
When Autumn's tints are glittering in the air,
That voice will whisper to his soul, "prepare;"
When Winter's snows are spread o'er knoll and dell,
"Oh this is death," that solemn voice will swell;
But when with Spring, streams leap and blossoms
    wave,
"Hope, Christian, hope," 'twill say, "there's life
    beyond the grave.

"Music followed from one of the bands on the ground—a solemn, funereal strain—in harmony with the vein of sentiment which ran through Mr. Street's admirable poem.

"The Hon. D. D. Barnárd here delivered the Address—an eloquent and finished production. His topics are appropriate, and are handled with his usual vigor and felicity. His vindication of the claims of the dead to a quiet and secure resting place, is admirable in sentiment, as it is strongly fortified by references to the usages and customs of nearly all nations, savage and civilized, and to the religious feelings of every Christian people."

The most agreeable time to linger here—at least so we think—is just after the evening sun peeps in over the western trees, upon the laughing fountain and the limpid lake, and drops a rainbow down to crown the entrancing picture.

Now if you wish to return to the entrance, you can effect your purpose by taking the *TOUR* easterly, past the capacious marble vault of HENRY YATES, which, by the way, is one of the oldest and most admirably located tombs in the place.

Another means of exit may be found in the meandering and leafy path called *MEDITATION WALK*, which leads from the southeast corner of the Lake, and, running high above the road along the face of the southern bluff, forms a most delightful, shady promenade.

We notice that the supply of water for *CONSECRATION LAKE* comes through the Ravine which extends from it westerly. *RAVINE WALK* pursues this stream and leads into the depths of the hollow pass spoken of, where the intense heat of a sultry summer's day never penetrates. *RAVINE SIDE*

WAY runs along its northerly side. This latter we will take, when we commence our examination of the central division of the grounds, of which the Ravine partially forms the southern boundary

MIDDLE RIDGE.

LEAVING *CONSECRATION LAKE* behind, and proceeding westerly into *RAVINE SIDE WAY*, we pass the lot of TAYLOR on the left. It contains a broken column. On the right is the soldier's monument to Col. EDWARD A. SPRINGSTEED, and next is the lot of SPALDING, containing two neat sculptured headstones.

We ascend past the small monuments of J. R. CUTLER, DAVID SMITH, and COBURN and RAWSON. At the junction of this road, with one diverging northeasterly, is the WENTZ monument, and and the monuments of J. C. KIRK and C. T. SMYTH.

Advancing still westerly, along the Ravine, we meet Ravine Bridge, and facing it, on our right, the highly polished memorial of the ORR family presents a front view. This is conspicuous, not alone through its generous size, its elegant finish, or its prominent location. Aside from these, the fact that it is the only polished shaft of native granite on the ground, lends to it that attractive-

Lith of G.W.Lewis 452 Broadway. Albany.

ness which any superior object, tending to conserve the ends of pleasing variety, ever possesses for the discriminating observer. This monument, which so admirably decorates its locality, can be seen to fine advantage from the opposite side of the bridge. The lot upon which it stands is also graced by a neat soldier's memorial to WM. EMMET ORR.

Next comes the several headstones in the lot of WILLIAM ORR, and then is seen the large oblong plat of one family of the VAN RENSSELAERS—relatives of that other famous Albany family of the same name, of which we have before spoken. The lot contains four prominent memorials — a handsome free-stone with cross, a rustic cross, and two good sized marble monuments, one of which bears the name of Gen. SOLOMON VAN RENS-SELAER, who was well known in this State and the city of Albany, by his civil and military position and services.

Of all the military heroes who have found sepulture here, not one, perhaps, has had a more eventful career than General VAN RENSSELAER. He commanded a troop before the age of twenty, and fought under "Mad Anthony" in the historic battle of Miami, upon which occasion he received a wound through the lungs which was declared to be mortal. Notwithstanding this decree, he won a speedy victory over the wound and the doctors, and was soon again ready for service. In the battle of Queenstown he was completely riddled with balls, and again survived. He afterwards held several important political positions, and died aged seventy-eight years.

A little distance west from VAN RENSSELAER is the granite of GEORGE H. THACHER. We pass the monument of BENDER, with Maltese cross, and the names of McCAFFERTY, CHAPMAN, and WANDELL are seen. Ahead is the monument of STEVENSON and DE WITT. The lot upon which this stands contains the remains of Hon. D. D. BARNARD, who delivered the consecratory address when these grounds were formally given to the dead.

We will curve round to the north, and ascending the hill before us, pass HOLMES, HURST, and

HASTINGS. Here is the neat cottage monument of BARENT SANDERS, and in the lot with it is a monumental headstone to MINNIE and KATIE. A niche in front of this pretty piece of sculpture contains two figures. Its emblems are various.

That figure of Grief seen upon our right, a little farther up the hill, surmounts the monument of ALLEN. A child, in the attitude of prayer, occupies a place on the front side. Opposite this is a circular lot, with two large brown-stone monuments, one of which displays the following inscription:

LEWIS N. MORRIS,

Brevet Major, U. S. A.,

Fell Sept. 21, 1846, at

MONTEREY,

In command of the 3d Regiment
United States Infantry,
While leading it
To the assault.

Erected by the citizens of
Albany, to commemorate
The gallantry of the soldier,
The worth of the man.

We turn westerly round Morris, and advancing, see the substantial marble of Fowler. Next ahead is Olcott's monument. It will reward a very careful study. That sculptured form which occupies the pedestal deserves our attention; but do not fail to observe, particularly, those expressive little figures, in relief, upon the front side of the stone. You apprehend their meaning—a mother rising towards her children, who have gone before, and who descend to meet and crown her from their angel home.

The headstone of Ransom is opposite Olcott, and in the same lot with this lies Edward C. Delavan, the great total abstinence agitator. He was connected with every prominent temperance movement in the world from 1832 up to the time of his death, which occurred in January, 1870. His communications upon his favorite hobby have reached nearly all the noted statesmen, physicians and philanthropists living. Among the celebrities who were interviewed by him on the temperance question were Louis Phillippe and the

Pope. After inaugurating his crusade against rum he proved his sincerity by emptying the costly wines in his own cellar into the street. He first became noted as a reformer while residing in Albany, in which city his large fortune was also acquired. That mammoth house, the "Delavan," in the city named, is a portion of the property which has fallen to his heirs.

On the left, again, are the MARVIN monument and sarcophagus, and opposite these is the lot of THOMAS W. OLCOTT, who, as you may be aware, has been President of the Albany Cemetery Association for more than a score of years.

The last statement suggests a digressive look backwards. The events of the last two decades have had their influence upon the affairs of this institution, as well as upon those of the outside world. The Albany Rural Cemetery was founded at a time when the idea of an extensive garden cemetery was comparatively new in this country. It was not always upon as solid a footing as at present, but in

7*

its infancy was obliged to struggle against the difficulties which, in those days, invariably beset all similar enterprises of any great magnitude. You would, perhaps, be pleased to know something of the details of its progress, and the causes of its existing prosperity; but as we are now ostensibly engaged simply in seeing it as it is, we will leave that subject for its future historian, and pursue our original purpose.

On our left is RAYMOND'S marble, and as we proceed, the granite temple to Dr. MARCH is noticed. We will soon take the descending road southerly, and westerly round MARCH; but first let us look about us, and contemplate the scenery on either side.

We are upon the narrowest part of the *MIDDLE RIDGE. INDIAN LAKE* looks up to us, through a leaf-fringed vista, from the guarded depths of the wild Ravine upon the north. This is the largest lake upon the grounds, and in time, no doubt, will be the finest. Near us, to the south, is *TAWASEN-THA*—the body of water which furnishes the head for the fountain that ruffles the bosom of its sister lake below.

Now we will move along towards *TAWASENTHA LAKE*, leaving MARCH upon our right. As we descend we notice in the distance, lining the bank south of the Lake, the tombs of PESTER and OSTERHOUT, CHARLES STANFORD, and BRINCKERHOFF and PUMPELLY. Near the Lake is the neatly coped lot of APPLETON, and farther east the massive granite monument, with polished tablets, of Gen. JOHN TAYLOR COOPER.

If we look sharply we will see, in the same line with the tombs before mentioned, a low block of marble inscribed "The Grave of the BRIDGENS," and some distance back of it a single undecorated grave. The simple quaintness of this inscription has provoked many a query, and yet there is nothing cabalistic in it. The grave contains the reinterred remains of several members of the BRIDGEN family. In its location does it not remind you of the poet's picture—

"Mine be the breezy hill that skirts the down,
  Where a green grassy turf is all I crave,
With here and there a violet bestrown,
  Fast by a brook or fountain's murmuring wave,
  And many an evening's sun shine sweetly on my
     grave."

Let us continue our descent to the foot of this slope, and look upon the monument of JOHN C. SPENCER, the illustrious lawyer and statesman, about whom Thurlow Weed tells an interesting political story in his "Experiences." His able revision of the statutes of this State — a task assigned to him by De Witt Clinton, shortly before the death of this remarkable personage — is, in itself, a sufficient monument.

AMBROSE SPENCER, the father of the subject of our previous remarks, also has a memorial in the same lot. He, too, was a distinguished lawyer and prominent politician.

Opposite SPENCER, on our right, and built in the face of the hill, is the DOUW vault. Can you decipher that faint inscription above the door — JOHN DE PEYSTER DOUW.

As we move along past DOUW, westerly, we see

to the left a sarcophagus of Quincy granite, supporting a large anchor in relief. This is the memorial of "Capt. ROBERT TOWNSEND, of the U. S. N., who died Aug. 16, 1866, at Chin Kiang, China, while in command of the U. S. steamer Wachusett." It is at once elegant, modest and substantial; and, inasmuch as it is entirely different from any other memorial here, it possesses no little attraction for the seeker after novelties.

Next to TOWNSEND is MARTIN'S large, heavy granite, with Grecian urn. We will now round up this steep slope past QUACKENBUSH, and, turning easterly into *WESTERN AVENUE*, stand before the HAMILTON monument. This is certainly one of the finest specimens of the unapproachable Gothic, of which these grounds can boast. That surmounting figure is Faith. The memorial looks down upon the grave of Col. DAVID HAMILTON, a gentleman of wealth and leisure who was well known among the public men of fifteen years ago, in Albany county and vicinity.

Our next advance will be easterly in the road

upon which we now stand. If we desired to leave
the Cemetery here, we might do so by taking the
westerly continuation of this avenue, past DAVIS,
WHARTON, ROY and the BOYDS, and on by the
cottages beyond to the western entrance. Near
the entrance are the church grounds, where lie the
re-interred dead of the abandoned grave yards of
Albany.

Whenever you feel like devoting a half day to
the object, we would advise you—especially if you
are a bit of an antiquarian—to go among these
transplantations of the great Reaper, and read—if
you can—the old inscriptions upon some of the
recumbent stones. There you will find samples of
the characteristic phraseology and orthography
of the last century. You will find hackneyed
churchyard epitaphs—some appropriate and affect-
ing, in spite of repetition; some evidently home-
brewed and thoroughly unimpressive, and some
unequivocally absurd. The many inscriptions in
German will recall your historical gleanings of the
days of Fort Orange and Rensselaerwyck; and the

instructive, practical contrast between these crude landmarks of the past and the evidences of the modern innovations of art and taste so near by, will more than reward the trouble of your visit.

But we are losing time. As we have already proposed, we will move easterly from HAMILTON. Here is the lot of JAMES ROY. Its principal adornment is a sarcophagus in marble.

We continue on past JOHN VAN ZANDT, EIGHTS, COBB, SCOTT, BOYD, GRAY and DEAN. To the left, the names of CHAPIN, CAMPBELL and HOFF-MAN appear. Again we see the memorial which preserves the name and features of Dr. MARCH. You remember that we left this on our right but recently, as we descended towards the Lake. If you have ever known the original, you will surely recognize in that medallion the American autocrat of surgery. We only learn from the stone before us that Dr. ALDEN MARCH lived and died. No labored eulogy perpetuates his deeds; nor is such tribute necessary. His fame is self-preserving.

The ensuing portion of this avenue we have

lately traversed for a short distance. We advance past the objects before seen, and, crossing the intersecting *Tour* beyond, leave the high cast iron enclosure and the monument of CHOLLAR and DUNHAM on our left.

To the right, ahead, is the marble mausoleum of MEADS. Here lies the philanthropic JOHN MEADS, an old and respected citizen of Albany, who was conspicuous in many noble public charities. During the latter years of his life he was the most frequent of visitors to these grounds and to this spot.

Now on, still in *WESTERN AVENUE,* easterly, past BROWN, HARRIS, ALLEN, FASSETT, ROBERTS and DANIELS. To the right is the monument of the WHITE brothers, and in the same lot a sarcophagus to ANDREW WHITE. We proceed by FORD, SMITH, WHITE and WILSON. This latter is on our right. Look at that pretty little headstone which the lot contains. Near here is an enclosed grave—a singular object.

Let us look to the left, towards GANSEVOORT—

an old and honored Albany name. The inscriptions upon that small stone to Brigadier-General PETER GANSEVOORT and wife, are interesting. Nearly one hundred years ago, General GANSEVOORT "defended Fort Stanwix against St. Leger, thereby preventing his junction with Burgoyne." "Here Stanwix' chief and brave defender lies." Behind the monument is a recumbent slab, inscribed to another GANSEVOORT, who in old times was one of the leading merchants of Albany. He died in the year 1800.

We again cross the *Tour*, leaving the hedge-enclosed lot of JOHN V. L. PRUYN upon our left, and proceeding past the WALDRON brown-stone to the monument and sarcophagus of EGBERT EGBERTS. Do you know who first harnessed power to the knitting frame in this country, and who was foremost in developing that important American industry, the knitting business? The stone before us preserves his name. Ask any resident of that "City of the Mills," which was the scene of his labors, to whom, more than to any

8

other one man, the present importance of the place as a manufacturing district is due, and your answer will doubtless be—"EGBERT EGBERTS."

Another advance shows the names of HOWLAND, ROUSSEAU and EASTON, HOLT, BALDWIN, LOBDELL and MENEELY. Here lies ANDREW MENEELY, whose name is known wherever bells are used throughout the world. Through his ingenuity was effected a complete revolution in the process of bell-making, and a branch of manufacture previously precarious was made to yield ample wealth and enviable reputation.

Opposite MENEELY we read the name of HITCHCOCK, and then come TUCKER, MATHER, HASWELL, WATERMAN, PLATT, LAWRENCE, WASHBURN, STEVENSON and CRANE and CROWNER. This portion of the grounds is popularly known as "The West Troy Ridge," for the reason that a great number of the prominent residents of the place named have here formed a sort of community of their own.

Let us turn sharply to the right, round section

post fifty-eight, and, leaving *WESTERN AVENUE,* notice the monuments of CAMPBELL, VIELE, AN-DREWS and McHARG. Now we look easterly along the *TOUR,* which has just been entered, and see the unpretending low granite monument to WILLIAM L. MARCY. Towards it let us advance. We will not presume to enlighten you upon the public history of the illustrious personage whose name it bears, for with that you are probably familiar; but there is a little narrative most pertinent to this occasion, which with your permission we will relate.

This central division of the grounds was purchased from WM. L. MARCY and others, executors of the estate of Benjamin Knower, by the Cemetery Association. It was then known as the Knower farm. Mr. MARCY was connected with the Knower family by marriage, and was in early life a frequent visitor to this rural retreat. This was some time before the idea of establishing a Rural Cemetery for Albany had taken any definite form. In after life he often alluded to the pleasure he had realized amid the quiet shades of this grand conservatory of nature's charms. To the very spot where now stands his memorial, he would regularly repair, alone, to indulge in solitary reflection; or, book in hand, to cultivate the acquaintance of a favorite author. The plat of ground which holds his ashes was purchased for him after his death, in consequence of its associations, and in accordance with the frequently expressed preference of the consummate statesman for this selection.

Before proceeding farther, let us look westerly along the crest of this bluff, and observe the Gothic monument to BENJAMIN KNOWER—the gentleman of whom we have spoken in the preceding paragraph. That was a leading name among the solid men of Albany some years ago. At the time of its erection, that monument was considered one of the finest here. It is yet much admired.

From MARCY we move easterly, past FOWLER and GIBBS. We are about to leave the *Tour*

again, and descend into *CRESCENT WAY;* but
first we will notice on the left the large marble
monument of SCHUYLER, and the brown-stone of
B. F. SMITH. This last named gentleman was
once a celebrated architect of Albany, and fur-
nished designs for many of the large and costly
monuments here.

As we move on, leaving ROBINSON'S free-stone
on our left, the marble of OTIS ALLEN is passed,
and now we look down from the rear upon BUR-
DEN'S vault, which we will soon approach in front.
At the next turn is a stately free-stone, profusely
inscribed. It is in itself an interesting history.
Among its inscriptions we read a name inseparably
associated with one of the greatest scientific institutions in the land. Who but has heard of that
well known public monument which stands an
enduring evidence of the munificence of that
revered lady, Mrs. BLANDINA DUDLEY?

Beyond the turn, and opposite DUDLEY, in the
VAN BUREN lot, is a chaste marble cross to
" Prince JOHN," and a three-sided brown-stone to

8*

the hardly less illustrious Judge VAN DER POEL.
An inscription upon the south side of the cross,
reads:

JOHN VAN BUREN,
SON OF
MARTIN AND HANNAH
VAN BUREN.

Born at Hudson, Feb. 10, 1810.

Died at sea, Oct. 13, 1866.

We will next turn from VAN BUREN northerly,
and, leaving behind the memorial of this latter-day
political celebrity, with whose public history you
are probably well acquainted, will pass BAKER and
BUCKBEE, and notice the soldier's monument to
Col. JOHN WILSON, another of the many martyrs
here who died to vindicate a glorious cause.

That exquisite tomb before us, with its watchful
canine guardians, may well arrest our attention.
It has doubtless called forth more of enthusiastic
admiration than any similar architectural production in this country. Casual visitors by the hundred—all unquestionably impartial, and many of

them fully competent to decide by comparison—
have conceded to the Albany Rural Cemetery the
possession of the model of side-hill tombs.

It is generally understood that this elaborate
sepulchre was, in its essential features, at least,
designed by Mrs. HENRY BURDEN, a lady of rare
gifts, who has for several years been one of its ten-
ants. Look upon the left hand page of that large
sculptured book, and read its poetical tribute to
her memory.

It is but recently that one of the most remarkable men of the age came here to join his beloved
consort in her eternal resting place. We will not
undertake to instruct you in detail concerning the
history of HENRY BURDEN. If you are familiar
with the annals of American enterprise and invention, you must necessarily be aware of his achievements. Of course you have heard of that wonderful machine which, as if born to meet a national
emergency, poured forth torrents of iron foot-gear
for our army horses during the late war. Then
there is the "Niagara of water wheels," as it has

been poetically termed. You know that this mammoth engine of the Wynantskill Valley has been considered a mechanical marvel by tourists and others, from all parts of the world, for nearly a quarter of a century. The talented clergyman of Troy, who delivered the funeral discourse upon Mr. BURDEN, pays him this tribute:

"With intellectual powers of a high order, a benignant providence endowed him with an inventive faculty so fertile in resources, and so varied in the practical workings, as to give in the great department of mechanical invention by which the elements of nature are combined, arranged and adjusted, important, new and useful results. The name of HENRY BURDEN will be associated with those of Cartwright and Whitney, Fulton and Morse, the products of whose genius are now found in every quarter of the civilized world."

The structures before us are not the only monuments which serve to perpetuate the BURDEN name. Cast a glance easterly, towards those fire-breathing manufactories beyond the Hudson.

Those are the BURDEN Mills. Less than one score years ago their present site was simply a swampy, unappropriated waste. The "Woodside" Church stands high among those distant eastern hills. If we should pay it a visit we might read, upon an elegant tablet within, this inscription: "Woodside Memorial Church, dedicated to the service of the Triune God, has been erected to the memory of HELEN BURDEN, in accordance with her long cherished and earnest desire, 1869." The church was erected by Mr. BURDEN not long before his death. From the charming villa of "Woodside," the BURDEN residence, which is located not far from the religious temple alluded to, the tomb beside us is plainly visible, although we cannot discern the former from here.

Now let us again advance. If we look northerly from BURDEN, we will notice, upon the ascending continuation of *CRESCENT WAY*, a very odd-looking combination of brown-stone and marble. It is the monument of OZIAS HALL. We will approach it, passing PECK and TRIPP.

The HALL structure attracts attention principally for the reason that it helps to gratify that human weakness—a love of variety. Because it does so, it should not, perhaps, be unfavorably criticised, for frequent repitition in monumental design is anything but desirable.

Let us call your attention to a lot opposite HALL, containing a rustic cross and three soldiers' headstones. Here lie the VAUGHN brothers— a Colonel, a Captain and a Private—three victims of the late rebellion, out of one household.

A little farther ahead, on the same side, we stop to glance at a small, but very pretty monument, to Capt. JOHN A. MORRIS, who fell mortally wounded, at the head of his command, near Spottsylvania Court House, on May 19, 1864.

We move ahead, curving and gradually ascending towards the top of the hill, without meeting any memorial of note. On our right is the rugged Ravine, which separates us from the *NORTH RIDGE*. As we accomplish the ascent, and strike the ubiquitous *TOUR* again, the nicely decorated

Lith of G.W. Lewis 452 Broadway, Albany.

ALEXANDER.

lot of J. W. MORANGE is seen upon the left, and
back of this the cross-crowned marble of FITCHETT.
In the same line with the last are the monuments
of LINEY and DANN, and then, as we proceed
westerly along the Ravine, the headstones of BEN-
NETT are observed.

Now several lots are passed before we reach the
monument of SILLIMAN, ALEXANDER and FINCH.
In the lot upon which this stands, there rests a
former wealthy and honored citizen of West Troy.
He was familiarly known as "Captain" SILLIMAN.
His high-toned estimate of what constitutes integ-
rity, and whole-souled abhorrence of the modern
tricks of trade, were his distinguishing characteristics. Although not injudiciously benevolent, he
was always prompt to help those who seemed disposed to help themselves. He proved, by amassing
an easy competence, always keeping in view the
rights of his fellow man, that trickery was not
essential to worldly success. He believed that a
man's word ought to be his bond, and he left a
record in accordance with that doctrine.

Before advancing much farther, we see Dell
Cross Bridge, which spans the Ravine to the right,
and opens communication from here with the
NORTH RIDGE. But let us postpone our inspection of that portion of the grounds for the present,
and turn sharply to the right into *DELL WOOD
AVENUE*—the alluring road which runs easterly
along the south side of the Ravine.

Now a pleasant five minutes' stroll will bring us
to the eastern limits of the Cemetery. As we move
along, we will narrate to you an interesting incident concerning that division of the grounds which
we have just reviewed.

The commission appointed to locate the State Lu-
natic Asylum, once visited what is now the *MIDDLE
RIDGE* of the Albany Rural Cemetery, and decided
that here should be the site of that Institution.
A prominent New York gentleman, named Wilber,
who was one of the commission, was particularly
enthusiastic in his praise of the location; and his
associates, among whom was the present President
of this Cemetery, unanimously concurred in the

opinion that the site was surpassingly eligible. Had it not been that some insuperable obstacle prevented the purchase of the grounds at that time, these lofty hills around would now answer back a mocking echo to the discordant shrieks of the madman, instead of listening in quiet sympathy to the whispered prayer or stifled sigh of those bereaved.

But we have emerged from the Ravine. As we reach the point where *DELLWOOD AVENUE* joins the *TOUR*, we see the Receiving Vault to the right. We have looked upon nearly every noteworthy object upon the *MIDDLE RIDGE*, and will now turn our attention to the Northern Division of the grounds.

9

NORTH RIDGE.

A S we stand near the Receiving Vault and glance northerly, we observe, upon an elevation beyond, the prominent edifice of JOHN F. WINSLOW. The *TOUR* will lead us to it. Let us advance and ascend. Moving along past the memorial of the MAYELL family, we proceed by COLBURN, SLASON, AGNEW, DANKER, McCALL and SCHWARTZ.

We have reached WINSLOW's Gothic chapel. This is by far the most .costly structure, of any kind, which these grounds contain, and its location is certainly one of the most desirable here. Its owner, as you may be aware, is a king among the great iron manufacturers of the country. Its material is of different varieties, but the enduring granite prevails. It has stood here now for many years; but you see, from the well-kept pebbled paths, the clean, close shaven sward, the general neatness of its surroundings, that with the lapse of time its interests are not forgotten.

You will probably commend this laudable pride;

RECEIVIN

ING VAULT.

but you may also ask how the future preservation
of this, or of any similar costly structure, can be
assured? Who will jealously guard it against
decay after its present owner shall have been
"resolved to earth again," and the nearest descendant of the third or fourth generation hence shall
have become apathetic as to the wishes of the former regarding it? We answer, that all deplorable
contingencies are forestalled by the Trust Fund
system, which places the remedy in the hands of
the original owner.

There are now in this Cemetery quite a number
of "funded" lots. A certain sum of money is de-
posited with the President of the Association, the
interest of which, or such portion of it as may be
necessary, is applied to the keeping the lot and its
accessories well preserved. The unexpended interest is allowed to accumulate to meet extraordinary
repairs—such, for instance, as the replacing of any
portion of a structure. This system is rapidly
gaining in favor, and its advantages will yet be
embraced by many lot owners here, who now, in

the flush of health and vigor, prefer to take care, personally, of their own cemetery property.

Again let us proceed. The *Tour* curves westerly as it approaches the WINSLOW edifice upon the south. We will leave this structure upon the right, and pass JOHN M. PECK and MOORE. Opposite is the oval pillar of CHAMBERS, and as we cross the Dell ahead, we pass COBB's vault and approach that of VISSCHER. Here the *Tour* winds suddenly towards the east, and, turning with it, we pass FISHER, SMITH, SLACK, McBURNEY and MURDOCK.

Now the *Tour* describes a regular curve, and we soon look upwards towards two monuments upon the northeast corner of the high bank to the left. One of these—the marble—bears a very suggestive inscription. It belongs to the STRAIN family. We will soon reach it.

Turning westerly, we skirt the bank of another, and the most northerly of those deep ravines, in the possession of which these grounds differ so favorably from the majority of cemeteries. We

soon see section post seventy-eight upon the right.
Here the direction of the *Tour* is again suddenly
reversed, and turning abruptly to the left, we proceed easterly towards the STRAIN monument, to
read that significant inscription before spoken of:
" FIRST INTERMENT AND MONUMENT IN THE
CEMETERY."

The first interment here perpetuated, was that
of DAVID STRAIN, aged twenty-one years, who was
interred in May, 1845. The population of this
place has increased wonderfully since that time.
If this person had lived on until our day — and
remember, he had already crossed the dividing line
between man and boy — he would be scarcely
beyond the meridian of life. He would still be
engaged in pursuing "his favorite phantom," as
we now pursue ours—would think the intervening
time merely a swift-winged shadow—would believe
his life only well begun—would anticipate new
triumphs, and would look forward, perhaps, to
many years of health and happiness; and yet how
very many have been garnered into this granary
9*

of death in the short period that has elapsed since his burial. One solitary mound here then—now, thousands upon thousands.

You will observe that the STRAIN monument well stands the wind and weather. Other succeeding memorials have completely succumbed to their destroying influences. Some have been rebuilt or repaired; but this still remains intact, without crack or flaw to vitiate its durability. It was erected by JOSEPH STRAIN, an old and prominent Albanian, who has since made his bed beside it. And in this connexion would it not be interesting to know who built the first monument here? That man was JOSEPH DIXON, who now lies upon the *SOUTH RIDGE*, and who was once an extensive marble manufacturer of Albany.

Now let us turn from this pioneer of the "Silent City," and observe the brown-stone of HIRAM PERRY. This variety of stone was once very popular here, and the place is adorned by some very fine free-stone monuments among the older erections. But human tastes change, like all things

in this changeable world, and now a free-stone is
seldom introduced.

Next to PERRY is the tall marble of MESICK,
and on our right are the elegant structures of
GOULD. That sarcophagus will probably bear
comparison with any similar memorial here.
Mark well the artistic excellence of that small
winged figure.

This swelling knoll is called *LANDSCAPE HILL.*
Now round GOULD, westerly, and on by LITTLE,
BORN, WESTERLO and the lot of JOHN DISNEY.
Farther on is' the draped marble of LOCKWOOD,
and just beyond, the *TOUR* turns southerly, bring-
ing us past the slender granite obelisk of JOHN
THOMAS.

On the left is one of the most neatly decorated
lots we have yet seen. Let us move to the front,
and upon the marble steps read the name of J. W
DUNHAM. That urn-guarded entrance we will
admire. Those pure white headstones are richly
wrought in emblematic flowers; and, better still,
real, living flowers, most scrupulously tended by

some careful hand, are lining the enclosure, and crowning that central mound. We do not often see a prettier picture.

Upon our right is a fine granite vault, and in front we look upon that sacred memento of our late national tribulation, the Soldiers' Ground. We will defer our observations upon this · until we approach it on the other side.

Let us move ahead in the *Tour*, crossing *Pine Grove Avenue*, until we stand beside section post seventy-four, and directly north of the soldiers' monument. Here *Buena Vista Turn* runs into the *Tour* from an easterly direction. We will leave the latter and take the first named road, because there is a monument at the turn below, to which we would direct your attention. A short walk brings in view BURT'S large marble—the object in question.

BURT'S was considered a noble structure once; and so it was—in appearance. You observe that it is giving out in all directions. That die is the weak point. It is fast crumbling away, and must

soon fail to support the heavy shaft above. It is
not a solid piece, as you discover at a glance, but
consists of four frail marble tablets, surrounding
an inner block of masonry. Those corner scrolls
have involved considerable labor in their execu-
tion. Pity that so much good work should have
been sacrificed to a single oversight!

We are on *ARBOR HILL*. Let us be sure and
not lose the strikingly picturesque view spread out
below and beyond. Not an elevation upon these
grounds lends to the vision greater scope, or presents a scene of rarer beauty. There is the tur-
reted iron mart of the Upper Hudson, visible to
its northernmost limits, with its dim background
of climbing peaks "buried in air" beyond. A
closer view brings within range an animated pan-
orama of smoke-wreathed steamers and multiform
sailing craft, upon the bosom of that grand estuary
of the Atlantic, made famous years ago by the
achievements of a Fulton. The eye now droops
from those distant glories, roves over cultivated
fields, or, nearer still, looks down upon the sloping

carpet of verdure, stretching away to the eastern limits of this last estate of man.

Now before advancing farther, permit us to give you our opinion of the merits of this part of the Cemetery. We believe it to be the finest division of these wonderfully diversified grounds. Where else can be found such alluring curves—such lofty, precipitous banks, and undulating roads—such deep ravines and swelling knolls—such charming vision of hill and dale—such a combination of the requisites that go to make up the grand and beautiful in landscape scenery.

After noticing the large granite below, of J. B. JERMAIN, we turn westerly, around BURT. Now the road gently rises, and passing BANCROFT, ALVORD, THOMAS, LEDDY, McDUFFIE and GILLESPIE, we again approach the Soldiers' Ground.

This great repository of the patriotic dead is marked by nearly one hundred and fifty mounds. That unfinished monument was intended to support a bust, in bronze, of Abraham Lincoln, and to be clothed in metallic tablets, which were to display the names of those who rest beneath those grassy heaps. For some unexplained reason it has never been completed, although that pedestal has stood there since February, 1870.

If those who were commissioned to rear a fitting memorial to Albany's bravest and best, have forgotten to pay an honest debt, the general public, certainly, have not forgotten the respect due their memory. Once a year these mounds are bestrown with floral offerings. Once a year the merchant leaves his counting room, the clerk his desk, the artisan his bench, the man of leisure his trifling employments, the servant her kitchen drudgery, the dainty lady her home comforts, and all join in doing homage over the turf that covers this silent colony of martyrs.

In approaching the Soldiers' Ground upon this side, we have again struck the *Tour*. We follow on, westerly, for some distance, without meeting any object of note. But now the large marble obelisk to HENDRICK HALLENBAKE attracts the eye. There are a number of other monuments in

the same lot, and their inscriptions show a diversity
of names. This is one of the most noticeable private
plats in the Cemetery. Noticeable, not on account
of any excess of artistic display, but because of an
indescribable something in its appearance which
tells us that it has a history. The name which
that large shaft bears is prominent in Albany annals, principally in consequence of the very cir-
cumstance which has here induced a number of
persons to make common cause. During the first
half of the last century, a portion of his farm was
appropriated by HENDRICK HALLENBAKE to the
purposes of a family burial ground. The ground
then set apart is now in the heart of Albany city,
although the removal to this Cemetery of the old
remains, some of which had been there for more
than a century, occurred as recently as the year
1860. Previous to this, for obvious reasons, the
ground had become undesirable as a burial place,
and, with the concurrence of the Legislature, the
property was sold for taxes by the order of John
O. Cole, Lewis Benedict, William Austin and

Alexander McHarg, who had been appointed trustees. It was purchased for these trustees for a period of a thousand years. They sold a portion of the property, and with a part of the proceeds bought this lot and that monument to HENDRICK HALLENBAKE. The above named trustees, with others, now own this lot.

From HALLENBAKE the *Tour* bears northerly, and in it we proceed by the marble of FONDA to the brown-stone of JOHN BRIDGFORD. You have heard of this noted builder before. His name has frequently been mentioned, of late, in connexion with that gigantic State enterprise, the Capitol, at Albany. Next to BRIDGFORD is the slender brown-stone of A. M. WHEELER, and opposite stands JONATHAN KIDNEY's small monument.

Here we are at *ARBOR WATER*, which we will leave on our left as we move on. This little lakelet is an artificial reservoir for the convenience of those lot owners in the vicinity who give personal attention to their own plants and flowers. The facilities afforded by it for procuring water, as

10

compared with the former lack of such an accommodation, will cause this little improvement to be highly appreciated.

Now we leave the *Tour*, turning northeasterly into *Union Avenue*, past section post eighty-six on our left. On every side are graded sections of eligible ground, which have recently been prepared for sale. We turn westerly round section eighty-six, into *Vernal Avenue*. We observe that the roads here are superior to those of any other portion of the grounds. They are broad, smooth, hard and gracefully curving.

Passing the Shaefer monument, we turn northerly into *Elm Wood Avenue*, past section post eighty-five, to our right. Let us move straight ahead, by section post eighty-four, and just beyond turn westerly. We pass Conly, and move on, still westerly, by the next section ahead to the left, which we will turn round southerly. But first let us glance to the north and observe the Public Lots. You understand that these lots are laid out in portions of a sufficient size to admit of a single interment. This arrangement is intended to accommodate those who either do not desire, or are unable to purchase a burial plat of greater dimensions. A portion of the public ground is specially designated the "Home of the Friendless." But very few of the graves in that monotonous plantation are distinguished by memorials. Occasionally a simple headstone tells the name of the sleeper beneath; and sometimes, too, a modest shrub, a small bouquet, or a few fresh flowers, bear testimony to the fact that the tenant of this grave, or that, is fondly remembered.

We turn now, to the left, leaving section post ninety-six on our right, and moving easterly into and along *WILD ROSE AVENUE.* The lot of G. W. KILBURN is passed, then the monument of the DOLE family and the memorials of ALEXANDER, LANSING, SIMPSON, HUGHES, TOWNSEND and BRAYTON.

To the left, on the corner, we see section post ninety-three. We turn in the opposite direction, southerly, and reach a portion of the *TOUR,* which

we pursue easterly, past WILBER, HINKLE, HET-
RICK and STORRS. That isolated lot, and monument in front, belong to WILLIAM SAWYER.

We again turn southerly, this time to the right,
and cross past the marble of PHILLIPS to still
another portion of the *TOUR*. The road slopes
easterly, and we descend by ANDERSON, COURT-
NEY, and the six-sided shaft of CHAPIN.

Here is Dell Bridge again. We will cross and
take *DELL WOOD AVENUE* once more, through
the Ravine, for we cannot finish our survey of
these grounds more delightfully than by moving
down this shady, sinuous passage towards the entrance. Before leaving the Bridge, however, let us
turn to the west and peer downward, through the
envious foliage, for a glimpse of *INDIAN LAKE*.

We have now traversed the avenue last named,
and will move round to the front side of the Receiving Vault. This is not the original structure.
The old vault was located near the entrance, in
the centre of the foregrounds. Although while it
stood it was found fully adequate to the demands

upon its capacity, it was unfavorably situated. This fact, together with the prospective necessity for a larger place of temporary deposit, to meet the fast increasing wants of the Cemetery in this direction, hastened the event of its demolition; and the structure before us was erected to supply its place, in the year 1858. In the selection of the present site of the Vault, the best of judgment was evinced. It is convenient to the entrance, and yet not too near. Although not an elegant structure, it is solid and substantial. It was constructed by John Bridgford, the noted Albany builder of whom we have previously spoken.

As we continue our progress towards the entrance, we see upon that hill to the right the large marble monument of SUMNER, CLARK and CORNELL, and then the oval memorial of VERNAM. Farther on, the stables are passed, and we look down upon the most easterly of the lakes. It is appropriately named *ORIENT LAKE*. That pretty, rustic house, which furnishes a home for the water fowl that animate the reservoir below, is neat

10*

enough for a rural cottage. But we can scarcely
say as much for that uncouth vault of brick,
above. If not a positive eyesore, it is far from
being ornamental, and it is consolatory to know
that the rules of this institution, as now administered, prohibit all additions to the present number
of such unsightly erections upon these grounds.

We have succeeded in pretty thoroughly explor-
ing the Albany Rural Cemetery, and now, before
reaching the end of this little manual, a few general observations, perhaps, will not be considered
obtrusive.

As far as the native merits of the "Rural" are
concerned, we will hazard the assertion that it is
not excelled in any one feature by any cemetery in
the country. On the other hand, it possesses all
those advantages which, individually or in pairs,
seem to form sources of congratulation to persons
interested in other institutions of the kind.

There are grounds devoted to the same purpose,

that combine all its diversity of topographical outline with a rocky, barren, uninviting exterior,
which this has not. Some are blessed with its
diversity and natural verdure, but lack its copious,
clear, perennial streams. Others, again, have its
abundance of water, its verdure, its unobjection-
able soil, but are without that charming combination of hill and dale, of scene and prospect, for
which it is pre-eminently distinguished. Many
like institutions may boast of their particular
advantages, but here is that approximation to in-
herent perfection which fully satisfies even the most
fatidious lover of the sublime and beautiful in
nature, and leaves nothing to be desired in the way
of adaptedness to the requisites of a burial place.

As a general thing it is difficult—especially
in the case of a person who is a lot owner in
Greenwood or in some similar place of equal pre-
tensions—to meet a stranger who is willing to
admit that the second oldest town in the Union
may possibly bury its dead in the first of Rural
Cemeteries—first in well founded claims to a lead-

ing place, we mean. There are exceptions, however, and now and then a visitor from a distance appears, who voluntarily sacrifices his home partialities to his honest convictions, and expresses himself accordingly.

We consider it a suggestive fact that a great number of the lot owners here are non-residents. Among these are persons living in New York, Chicago, Cincinnati and other localities, which, as far at least as this class of institutions is concerned, have no affinity whatever for Albany.

Now, how many persons go from this vicinity to New York, Chicago or Cincinnati to select a burial site? And why is it that proprietary interests are held in our Cemetery by those who would certainly purchase nearer home if personal convenience alone was consulted? We believe that the anomaly finds its explanation in the attractions of the place itself—in the irresistible allurements of its ever-varying landscape—in the many beauties that unite to make up the sum total of its expressive scenery.

EPITOME OF THE ROUTE.

TOUR, between 1* and 2, to *MOUNT WAY.*

MOUNT WAY, between 3 and 4, to *TOUR.*

TOUR, between 3 and 5, to *GLEN CROSS WAY.*

GLEN CROSS WAY, between 5 and 6, to *TOUR.*

TOUR, between 6 and 7, thence round 39, to *PROS-PECT AVENUE.*

PROSPECT AVENUE, by 37, on left, to *WILD FLOWER AVENUE.*

WILD FLOWER AVENUE, between 34 and 35, to *TOUR.*

TOUR, between 31 and 32, to *PROSPECT AVENUE.*

PROSPECT AVENUE, between 30 and 31, to *TOUR.*

TOUR, between 30 and 33, thence between 26 and 43, to *SPRUCE AVENUE.*

SPRUCE AVENUE, between 25 and 43, to *TOUR.*

TOUR, between 25 and 44, thence between 21 and 24, thence between 21 and 22, thence between 18 and 21, to *LAWN AVENUE.*

---

* The figures denote the sections on the map.

LAWN AVENUE, between 20 and 21, thence between 15 and 21, thence between 14 and 15, thence between 13 and 15, to *GREENWOOD AVENUE.*

GREENWOOD AVENUE, between 8 and 12, to *ROSELAND WAY.*

ROSELAND WAY, between 9 and 12, to *TOUR.*

TOUR, between 11 and 12, to *OAK FOREST WAY.*

OAK FOREST WAY, between 12 and 19, thence between 17 and 18, to *GREENWOOD AVENUE.*

GREENWOOD AVENUE, between 16 and 18, to *TOUR.*

TOUR, between 16 and 20, thence between 15 and 16, to *GREENWOOD AVENUE.*

GREENWOOD AVENUE, between 8 and 13, to *TOUR.*

TOUR, between 6 and 8, thence between 6 and 9, thence between 3 and 10, by *CONSECRATION LAKE*, to *RAVINE SIDE WAY.*

RAVINE SIDE WAY, between 56 and 57, to *TOUR.*

TOUR, between 54 and 56, to *WESTERN AVENUE.*

WESTERN AVENUE, between 53 and 54, to *TOUR.*

TOUR, between 52 and 54, to *HEMLOCK AVENUE.*

HEMLOCK AVENUE, between 45 and 52, to *WEST-ERN AVENUE.*

WESTERN AVENUE, between 50 and 52, thence between 53 and 54, thence between 55 and 56, thence between 58 and 59, to *TOUR.*

TOUR, between 59 and 62, thence between 61 and 62, to *CRESCENT WAY.*

CRESCENT WAY, between 61 and 62, thence between 60 and 61, to *TOUR.*

TOUR, between 59 and 60, thence between 53 and 60, to *DELL WOOD AVENUE.*

DELL WOOD AVENUE, between 60 and 65, thence between 64 and 65, to *TOUR.*

TOUR, between 65 and 66, thence between 71 and 72, thence between 70 and 73, thence between 70 and 76, thence between 76 and 77, thence between 76 and 80, thence between 73 and 75, to *BUENA VISTA TURN.*

BEUNA VISTA TURN, between 73 and 74, to *TOUR.*

TOUR, between 73 and 75, thence between 75 and 87, to *UNION AVENUE.*

UNION AVENUE, between 81 and 86, to *VERNAL AVENUE*.

VERNAL AVENUE, between 85 and 86, to *ELM WOOD AVENUE*.

ELM WOOD AVENUE, between 85 and 88, thence between 84 and 94, thence between 94 and 95, to *MEADOW AVENUE*.

MEADOW AVENUE, between 93 and 95, thence between 93 and 96, to *WILD ROSE AVENUE*.

WILD ROSE AVENUE, between 92 and 93, thence between 92 and 94, to *TOUR*.

TOUR, between 88 and 89, to *TOUR CROSS WAY*.

TOUR CROSS WAY, between 87 and 89, to *TOUR*.

TOUR, between 73 and 90, to *DELL WOOD AVENUE*.

DELL WOOD AVENUE, between 60 and 65, to *TOUR*.

TOUR, past Receiving Vault, thence to entrance.

APPENDIX.

EMBLEMS.

THE idea of closing this little work with a short appendix, touching upon emblems, was incidentally suggested to the writer of these pages, and had no direct connexion with his original design.

To those who are well versed in symbolical language, it will doubtless seem absurd to assume that a great number of persons, otherwise intelligent, are unacquainted with the meaning of the emblems in common use in our cemeteries. But we have the most indisputable evidence that such is the fact. Walk with us through the "Rural," and we will show you a dozen proofs.

In one instance, here, a full blown rose is wrought upon the memorial of a little child. Again can be seen a rose-bud among the emblems of a headstone which marks the resting place of

11

an old lady who lived to count her three-score and ten, if we may believe the inscription. Other cases show a still greater deviation from propriety.

In the instance first cited, the misapplication can neither be attributed to a lack of means, nor of ordinary intelligence, on the part of the lot owner. He is a gentleman well to do, and a person who could, if he chose, make time to investigate the emblem question whenever circumstances might intimate the necessity.

If the rearing of ornamental memorials were of frequent occurrence with each individual, it is probable that the signification of emblematic devices would be better understood; but as this is not the case, it is seldom that the subject is thought worthy of much attention. Especially does this remark apply to the busy man of the world, who, being ardently engaged "in the struggle for power or the scramble for pelf," never thinks of studying up matters of so little apparent importance. Now, why not consider the "eternal fitness of things" in the erection of a memorial, however small, as

well as in the building of a house, or in the execu-
tion of any other project? If "whatever is worth
doing is worth doing well," we think that the
adornments of the grave are fully entitled to the
benefit of the maxim.

In seeking an explanation of the abuses to which
we have called attention, we were curious enough
to interview several prominent dealers in stone,
upon the question. Our inquiries tended to show
that a great number of those who purchase memorials have not the faintest conception of what is
appropriate. Sculptured flowers and figures are
considered by them merely as ornaments, without
any regard to their symbolical relations. The result of this frequently is, that a stone is selected
simply because it is handsomely embellished, and
the age of the person whose memory it is intended
to preserve, is never taken into consideration.

The fault may sometimes be attributable to that
eminently human failing, a disposition to imitate.
For instance, a person loses a child and wishes to
adorn its grave with some pretty design, in stone.

The first step is to look over the cemetery. The most attractive specimen is sought as a model, rather than the most suitable; and the consequence is, that a garland in which the principal emblems are acorns with oak leaves, or some other device equally unsuitable for a child, will often be found contradicting an inscription below.

It may be urged that a conscientious dealer would guard the purchaser against such improprieties as those spoken of. Some do this, no doubt, but as a general thing we must consider that it is the business of the former to sell his wares, rather than to teach æsthetics. As the world goes, it would perhaps be unreasonable to expect him to interfere with the decision of his patron, if by so doing he incurred the risk of losing a good sale.

We have been unable to discover that any printed work, devoted exclusively to an exposition of the meaning of emblems, is procurable. The reason probably is, that the subject cannot easily be amplified to the dimensions of a book. We have a reliable reference in the Encyclopedia. But

in this work the names of the flowers and figures
used as types of idea and sentiment are not classi-
fied; and it requires a tedious search to glean
much information in the direction indicated, from
such sources. The poetical " Language of flowers "
gives some little insight into the matter; but its
definitions are too vague and general to afford
much that is practically available in the way of
instruction. For the sake of illustration, we
quote:

" In Eastern lands they talk in flowers,
  And they tell in a garland their loves and cares;
Each blossom that blooms in their garden bowers,
  On its leaves a mystic language bears.

     *   *   *   *   *

" Innocence dwells in the lily's bell,
  Pure as a heart in its native heaven;
Fame's bright star and glories swell
  By the glossy leaf of the bay are given.

" The silent, soft and humble heart
  In the violet's hidden sweetness breathes,
And the tender soul that cannot part,
  A twine of evergreens fondly wreathes.

" The cypress that darkly shades the grave,
  Is sorrow that mourns its bitter lot;
And faith that a thousand ills can brave,
  Speaks in thy blue leaves, ' Forget-me-not.' "

11*

The necessary limits of a Hand Book, which is designed to be small enough for convenience, require that we should refrain from enlarging too extensively upon this supplementary topic. As we believe that this book has already reached those limits, we will conclude with a short list of emblems, with their meanings. The list comprises some of those most frequently misapplied.

Rose-bud: Morning of life.

Morning Gloria: Beginning of life.

Butterfly: Short lived—an early death.

Full-blown Rose: Prime of life.

Lily: Emblem of innocence and purity.

Palm branch: Emblem of victory and rejoicing.

Ivy: Friendship and immortality.

Laurel: Emblem of fame or victory. It is found about the Mediterranean, and was early used to crown the victor in the games of Apollo.

Oak leaves and Acorn: Maturity, or a ripe old age.

Weeping Willow: Emblem of sorrow.

Corn: Ripe old age.

Sheaf of Wheat: Ripe for the harvest.

Poppy: Emblem of sleep.

Lotus: Emblem of sleep.

Lamb: Emblem of innocence.

Dove: Emblem of innocence, gentleness and affection. In scripture it is used as the typical emblem or symbol of the Holy Ghost.

Cherub: Angelic. A symbolical figure frequently mentioned in scripture, and used as a part of the embellishment of the tabernacle.

American Eagle: Surrounded by the stars and stripes, signifying eternal vigilance and universal liberty.

Hour Glass: With wings of time attached, representing time flying—shortness of life.

Cross: Emblem of faith.

Anchor: Emblem of hope.

Broken Ring: The family circle severed.

Broken Column: The head of the family.

Torch inverted: Life extinct.

Urn, with blaze: Undying friendship.

Harp: Praise to the Maker.

INDEX.

NAME.	SECTION.	LOCATION.	PAGE.
Adams Amos	3	Mount Way	12
Alden Stephen	3	Mount Way	11
Alexander Andrew & others.	59	Bower Hill	95
Allen Thomas W	5	Glen Cross Way	23
Allen Henry A	56	Western Avenue	75
Allen Hiram W	55	Western Avenue	84
Allen Otis	61	Crescent Way	89
Alvord Mary E	74	Arbor Hill	106
Amsdell George I	21	Sunset Lawn	47
Amsdell Theodore M.	21	Sunset Lawn	47
Anderson Family	73	Glen Wood Hill	112
Anderson George	42	Roseleaf Avenue	43
Anderson Absalom	43	Tour	45
Andrews William	7	Evergreen Path	25
Andrews Joel W	56	Tour	87
Angel at the Sepulchre	37	Prospect Hill	32
Appleton William	19	Tawaseutha Lake	79
Armsby J. H. Dr	9	Roseland Hill	53
Austin J	21	Lawn Avenue	48
Austin J. J	21	Lawn Avenue	48
Baldwin Ephraim, heirs of..	59	Western Avenue	86
Bancroft John and Joseph ..	74	Arbor Hill	106
Barnard D. D. and others...	56	Tour	74
Bayeux Thomas	16	Tour	57
Bay William Dr	15	Tour	58
Becker Storm A	40	Evergreen Path	47
Beebe Thomas F	44	Evergreen Path	46
Benedict Uriah, estate of....	3	Mount Olivet	16
Benedict J. and E. G	37	Greenleaf Forest	27
Bender William M	30	Cypress Water	41
Bender C. W. and others....	56	Tour	74
Bennett Ellen	59	Bower Hill	95

9

NAME.	SECTION.	LOCATION.	PAGE.
Bishop Frederick and Henry	15	Tour	57
Blakely and Johnson	39	Evergreen Wood	26
Bleecker James	3	Mount Way	12
Bleecker G. V. S., heirs of	3	Mount Way	12
Bleecker Harmanus	8	Mount Olivet	22
Born J. O.	77	Landscape Hill	103
Boyle Arthur	14	Evergreen Path	46
Boyd Family	51	Western Avenue	82
Boyd Robert	52	Western Avenue	83
Brainard Benjamin C.	13	Greenwood Avenue	51
Bridgford John	87	Tour	100
Bridgens, Grave of the	18	Tawasentha Lake	79
Brinckerhoff and Pumpelly	18	Tawasentha Lake	79
Britton Winchester	8	Tour	60
Brown Eleanor	56	Western Avenue	84
Brumaghim Albert M.	30	Cypress Water	41
Buckbee James A.	21	Sunset Lawn	47
Bullions Peter	16	Highland Water	57
Burden's Tomb	61	Crescent Glade	91
Burhans L.	15	Tour	57
Burt Family	74	Arbor Hill	104
Callender David	7	Tour	15
Campbell J. N. Rev.	41	Evergreen Wood	44
Campbell Archibald	18	Greenwood Avenue	55
Campbell Sarah	56	Tour	87
Carroll Howard Col.	33	Cypress Water	41
Carroll and Quackenbush	52	Hemlock Avenue	81
Cary John	21	Lawn Avenue	48
Chambers William	72	Tour	100
Chapin Ogden N.	50	Western Avenue	83
Chapin Lyman	73	Glen Wood Hill	112
Chapman Isaac	56	Tour	74
Chase L. A.	15	Tour	57
Chollar and Dunham	55	Beminden Hill	84
Clapp Reuel	6	Glen Cross Way	23
Clark James	5	Mount Olivet	22
Clark A. S.	21	Lawn Avenue	48
Cobb Eliza C.	15	Highland Water	58
Cobb J. N.	52	Western Avenue	83

131

NAME.	SECTION.	LOCATION.	PAGE.
Cobb Benjamin F	70	Tour	100
Colburn Robert	57	Ravine Side Way	72
Colburn Peter	65	Tour	98
Coleman James R	41	Forest Avenue	44
Collins Lorenzo D	5	Glen Cross Way	23
Conklin Lucy	33	Prospect Hill	40
Conly George P	95	Elm Wood Avenue	110
Cook Samuel H	34	Wild Flower Avenue	31
Cook William J	15	Tour	57
Cooper Heber T	44	Tour	45
Cooper John T. Gen	19	Tawasentha Lake	79
Corning Erastus	31	Prospect Hill	32
Couldwell Henry J	41	Forest Avenue	44
Coulson Thomas	5	Mount Olivet	19
Courtney Family	73	Glen Wood Hill	112
Cowell and Hulse	20	Lawn Avenue	48
Cox James	14	Evergreen Path	46
Crane and Crowner	59	Western Avenue	86
Crannell John W	4	Summer Hill	15
Crapo C. V	5	Mount Olivet	15
Crawford Samuel	3	Mount Olivet	16
Crocker Mason J	4	Summer Hill	15
Cruttenden Robert H	18	Greenwood Avenue	56
Cunliff Simeon	41	Evergreen Wood	43
Cunningham Ichabod L	13	Greenwood Avenue	60
Cutler J. R	57	Ravine Side Way	72
Cushman C. B. and R. S	16	Tour	57
Daniels Warner	56	Western Avenue	84
Danker Frederick	66	Tour	98
Dann Horace	59	Bower Hill	95
Davidson Anna	5	Mount Olivet	15
Davis Joseph	11	Roseland Hill	54
Davis John	51	Western Avenue	82
Dawson George	33	Cypress Water	42
Dean Amos	52	Western Avenue	83
De Forest Charles A	7	Forest Avenue	26
Delavan Edward C	53	Western Avenue	76
Dempsey John	16	Tour	57
Dennison Isaac	18	Greenwood Avenue	56

NAME.	SECTION.	LOCATION.	PAGE.
De Witt William H	4	Mount Olivet	13
Dey Ermand and Spellman	16	Greenwood Avenue	55
Dickerman John S	21	Sunset Lawn	47
Dickson Walter	37	Prospect Avenue	27
Disney John	77	Landscape Hill	103
Doncaster Daniel	8	Tour	61
Douw John D. P	52	Hemlock Avenue	80
Dudley Blandina Mrs	61	Crescent Way	89
Dunham John W	76	Pine Grove Avenue	103
Dunlop Robert	9	Roseland Hill	54
Durant Clark	5	Mount Olivet	14
Dyer David Rev	8	Mount Olivet	23
Edson Cyrus	15	Lawn Avenue	49
Egberts Egbert	58	Western Avenue	85
Eights Abraham	52	Western Avenue	83
Ellery John	21	Sunset Lawn	47
Elmendorf and Stevens	21	Sunset Lawn	47
Emblems			121
Esmay Isaac	15	Lawn Avenue	51
Evertson Jacob Jr	13	Greenwood Avenue	13
Fairburn John	42	Roseleaf Avenue	43
Fassett Timothy Mrs	56	Western Avenue	84
Featherly John Jr	20	Tour	56
Feltman J. C. and W. P	20	Lawn Avenue	47
Fish Artemus	5	Mount Olivet	14
Fish Samuel N	5	Mount Olivet	15
Fisher Joseph	76	Landscape Hill	100
Fitchett Henry	59	Bower Hill	95
Ford Eliakim W	44	Evergreen Path	46
Ford Philip	56	Western Avenue	84
Forsyth R	11	Ravine Cross Way	54
Fowler William	54	Western Avenue	76
Fowler and Gibbs	59	Tour	88
Frellegh and Snyder	7	Evergreen Path	24
Frisby Edward Col	20	Tour	56
Fry Daniel	8	Greenwood Avenue	60
Gannon P. Dr	3	Mount Way	13
Gansevoort Peter	55	Western Avenue	84
Gladding Joseph	21	Sunset Lawh	47

NAME.	SECTION.	LOCATION.	PAGE.
Godson and Blakeley	39	Evergreen Wood	26
Goodwin Albert	18	Greenwood Avenue	55
Gould Anthony and William.	77	Landscape Hill	103
Gower William H.	16	Tour	57
Grant and Company	5	Mount Olivet	15
Gray George F.	18	Greenwood Avenue	56
Gray Alexander and William	52	Western Avenue	83
Greer Alexander	39	Forest Avenue	26
Gregory Family	3	Mount Olivet	13
Groesbeck Catharine	44	Evergreen Path	46
Guest Sidney	8	Tour	61
Gunsalus and Perrigo	44	Tour	45
Hadley James R.	13	Prospect Avenue	26
Hallenbeck Mathew I.	5	Mount Olivet,	19
Hallenbake Hendrick	73	Tour	107
Hall John T.	3	Mount Olivet.	19
Hall Green,	8	Greenwood Avenue	60
Hall Ozias	61	Crescent Way	93
Hamilton Catharine	5	Mount Olivet.	15
Hamilton Samuel	15	Tour	58
Hamilton David	52	Western Avenue	81
Harris Edward A.	4	Mount Way	13
Harris James B.	56	Western Avenue	84
Hastings Seth	54	Tour	75
Haswell Joseph	59	Western Avenue	86
Hawley Cyrus	10	Roseland Hill	54
Hetrick Michael	89	Tour	112
Hillhouse John	4	Mount Way	12
Hillhouse Thomas	4	Mount Way	12
Hills John J	12	Greenwood Avenue	59
Hinckley Frederick	89	Tour	112
Hitchcock Isaac	59	Western Avenue	86
Hoffman Benjamin	50	Western Avenue	83
Holmes P. W.	15	Lawn Avenue	48
Holmes Isabella	54	Tour	74
Holt Jared	58	Western Avenue	86
Howe and Lloyd,	12	Roseland Way	51
Howe and Monteath	5	Glen Cross Way	15
Howland Susan M.	58	Western Avenue	86

12

Name.	Section.	Location.	Page.
Hoyt George A	3	Chapel Grove	11
Hulse and Cowell	20	Lawn Avenue	48
Humphrey Friend	3	Mount Olivet	21
Humphrey Hugh	6	Glen Cross Way	23
Hun Thomas	17	Greenwood Avenue	55
Hurst William	54	Tour	74
Irwin Wm. P. and D. W	41	Roseleaf Avenue	44
Jagger Ira	5	Mount Olivet	14
James Edward	7	Tour	15
James Family	16	Tour	58
Jeffers Thomas C	34	Wild Flower Avenue	31
Jermain J. B	65	Dell Side Avenue	106
Johnson and Schoolcraft	5	Mount Olivet	22
Johnson David J	40	Evergreen Path	47
Jones E. Darwin	37	Prospect Avenue	29
Jones James D	21	Lawn Avenue	48
Jones C. A	15	Lawn Avenue	48
Kane John I	5	Mount Olivet	22
Keeler Isaac N	40	Forest Avenue	44
Kelly Charles W	32	Prospect Hill	30
Kendrick E. E	4	Mount Way	13
Kennedy John Jr	40	Evergreen Path	47
Kidd, Ten Broeck and others	12	Greenwood Avenue	59
Kidney Jonathan	75	Tour	109
King Rufus	32	Prospect Hill	31
King Robert H	18	Greenwood Avenue	56
Kirk J. C	56	Ravine Side Way	72
Knower Benjamin	62	Oak Bough Avenue	88
Knowlton Myron B	21	Lawn Avenue	48
Lansing Joseph A	5	Mount Olivet	23
Lansing Anna	21	Lawn Avenue	48
Lathrop Dyer, heirs of	11	Roseland Hill	54
Lawrence Geo. H	59	Western Avenue	86
Lawyer David W	40	Forest Avenue	44
Learned B. P. and W. L	11	Roseland Hill	54
Leddy P. B. Mrs	75	Arbor Hill	106
Liney John	59	Bower Hill	95
Little Weare C	76	Landscape Hill	103
Lockwood John E	77	Landscape Hill	103

135

NAME.	SECTION.	LOCATION.	PAGE.
Lobdell Family	58	Western Avenue	86
Long and Silsby	16	Tour	57
Many William V	5	Mount Olivet	15
March Alden Dr	52	Western Avenue	83
Marcy William L	62	Tour	87
Martin James	16	Greenwood Avenue	56
Martin David Dr	15	Tour	58
Martin James	45	Hemlock Avenue	81
Marvin Alexander	54	Western Avenue	77
Muscraft William	35	Prospect Avenue	30
Mather Heman	58	Western Avenue	86
Mayell Jefferson	65	Tour	98
McBurney E	76	Landscape Hill	100
McCafferty Michael	56	Tour	74
McCall Patrick M. and others	66	Tour	98
McCammon Charles	5	Mount Olivet	21
McClasky Ja's and Jeanette	37	Prospect Avenue	27
McClure James	3	Mount Way	13
McClure Archibald	35	Prospect Avenue	28
McCredie Thomas	40	Forest Avenue	44
McElroy William	19	Ravine Cross Way	54
McElroy Henry	16	Greenwood Avenue	56
McHarg William	56	Oak Bough Avenue	87
McIntyre Archibald	9	Roseland Hill	53
McMillan James	44	Evergreen Path	46
McMullen Thos	5	Glen Cross Way	23
McNaughton Peter	5	Mount Olivet	14
Meads John	56	Western Avenue	84
Meech Henry T	12	Roseland Way	52
Meneely Andrew	58	Western Avenue	86
Merrifield William J	21	Lawn Avenue	48
Mesick Henry T	76	Landscape Hill	103
Miller Charles	4	Summer Hill	15
Miller W. Starr Mrs	29	Prospect Hill	34
Mitchell William	13	Greenwood Avenue	60
Mix Family	16	Tour	57
Monteath Wm. and Peter	35	Wild Flower Avenue	30
Monteath and Howe	5	Glen Cross Way	15
Moore William	71	Sunrise Lawn	100

NAME.	SECTION.	LOCATION.	PAGE.
Moore William and John....	21	Lawn Cross Way........ ..	47
Morange James W.........	59	Bower Hill.................	95
Morris Lewis N. Major......	54	Western Avenue............	75
Morris John A. Capt.......	60	Crescent Way............	94
Morrow James.............	8	Roseland Way.	52
Mosher Alfred..............	18	Greenwood Avenue........	55
Mount David..............,	39	Evergreen Wood...........	26
Muir William...............	6	Mount Olivet............	25
Munson Stephen............	42	Roseleaf Avenue............	43
Murdock Andrew...........	76	Landscape Hill..............	100
Nelson Alexander Dr.......	34	Wild Flower Avenue.......	31
Nessle Caroline G...........	5	Mount Olivet...............	19
Newland John..............	4	Mount Way.................	13
Newman Henry.............	6	Glen Cross Way............	23
Newton Mrs................	12	Oak Forest Way............	54
Newton William............	11	Roseland Hill..............	54
Northrop John G...........	37	Prospect Avenue...........	29
Noyes Edgar W............	40	Evergreen Path............	47
Olcott Thomas..............	54	Western Avenue...........	76
Olcott Thomas W..........	53	Western Avenue...........	77
Orr Family.................	56	Ravine Side Way...........	72
Orr William................	56	Ravine Side Way..........	73
Osborne Nehemiah.........	13	Evergreen Path............	47
Oswald Jane.............. .	5	Mount Olivet.....	21
Owens Edward..............	16	Greenwood Avenue........	56
Packard Chester............	21	Lawn Avenue..............	48
Page John E................	41	Forest Avenue..............	44
Parsons L. Sprague........	11	Roseland Hill..............	53
Patten Moses..............	3	Chapel Grove..............	10
Payn Benjamin..............	7	Evergreen Path............	24
Peckham Rufus W. and G.W.	11	Roseland Hill..............	54
Peck and Tripp..............	60	Crescent Way..............	93
Peck John M................	71	Sunrise Lawn..............	100
Perry Eli...................	5	Mount Olivet...............	23
Perry Hiram................	76	Landscape Hill.............	102
Pester and Osterhout.......	18	Tawasentha Lake...........	79
Phillips John................	89	Bramble Copse Walk.......	112
Phillips Levi................	5	Mount Olivet...............	20
Platt Jacob.................	59	Western Avenue............	86

Name.	Section.	Location.	Page.
Pohlman Charles	3	Mount Olivet	19
Pohlman H. N. Rev	6	Mount Olivet	24
Pomfret James E. Mrs	3	Mount Olivet	23
Porter Giles W	16	Tour	57
Pratt Geo. W. Col	44	Evergreen Path	46
Prentice Ezra P	7	Evergreen Path	24
Pruyn John V. L	59	Western Avenue	85
Public Lots	98	Meadow Avenue	110
Quackenbush Henry Col	9	Roseland Way	52
Quinn Michael	44	Tour	45
Ransom Samuel H	15	Lawn Avenue	51
Rathbone Joel	3	Chapel Grove	10
Rathbone Jared L	3	Chapel Grove	13
Rawson T. R	57	Ravine Side Way	72
Raymond Benjamin C	54	Western Avenue	78
Read and Spellman	11	Roseland Hill	54
Remond Narcisse	8	Tour	60
Rice Gen'l	42	Evergreen Wood	43
Richardson James	4	Summer Hill	15
Ridder T. B. Mrs	41	Evergreen Wood	44
Roberts Azor C	55	Western Avenue	84
Robinson and Cook	7	Evergreen Path	25
Robinson Samuel	12	Roseland Way	51
Robinson Edward	16	Greenwood Avenue	55
Roessle Theophilus	41	Evergreen Wood	44
Rogers Nelson	7	Tour	15
Rogers John	8	Tour	60
Root Lyman	39	Forest Avenue	27
Rose David	7	Prospect Avenue	25
Rossman John B. Dr	43	Roseleaf Avenue	43
Rousseau and Easton	59	Western Avenue	86
Roy John F. and Peter	45	Western Avenue	82
Roy James	52	Western Avenue	83
Safford Nathaniel	4	Summer Hill	14
Sague Samuel	14	Lawn Avenue	49
Salisbury Daniel	33	Greenleaf Forest	41
Sanders James B	54	Tour	75
Sanford Giles	6	Mount Olivet	25
Sanford George	18	Greenwood Avenue	55

138

NAME.	SECTION.	LOCATION.	PAGE.
Sawyer William	89	Arbor Water	112
Schaeffer Margaret	85	Vernal Avenue	110
Schuyler Philip Gen'l	29	Prospect Hill	34
Schuyler Samuel	59	Tour	89
Schwartz Frederick	65	Tour	98
Scott John	52	Western Avenue	83
Sedan Charles	13	Prospect Avenue	26
Seymour Eliza B. Mrs	11	Oak Forest Way	53
Seymour Family	18	Greenwood Avenue	56
Sheldon Gaylor	5	Mount Olivet	19
Sheppard William	12	Greenwood Avenue	51
Sherwood William H	33	Prospect Hill	40
Shonts John A	5	Mount Olivet	15
Silsby and Long	16	Tour	57
Slack Jacob	43	Spruce Avenue	45
Slack Harriet	76	Landscape Hill	100
Slason E. B. Mrs	65	Tour	98
Slingerland Ann B	3	Mount Way	13
Smith Daniel	7	Tour	15
Smith William	5	Mount Olivet	16
Smith Theodore D	40	Evergreen Path	47
Smith D. A	15	Lawn Avenue	48
Smith David	57	Ravine Side Way	72
Smith Isaac	55	Western Avenue	84
Smith B. F	59	Tour	89
Smith Ann	76	Landscape Hill	100
Smyth Charles T	56	Ravine Side Way	72
Snyder and Freliegh	7	Evergreen Path	24
Soldiers' Monument	75	Arbor Hill	106
Spaulding and Robins	62	Ravine Side Way	72
Spellman and Reed	10	Roseland Hill	54
Spellman and Dey Ermand	16	Greenwood Avenue	55
Spencer John C	45	Hemlock Avenue	80
Springsteed Edward A. Col.	62	Ravine Side Way	72
Staats John L	21	Sunset Lawn	47
Staats Peter P	21	Sunset Lawn	47
Stackpole John	43	Tour	45
Stanford Charles	18	Tawasentha Lake	79
Steele Lemuel	5	Mount Olivet	21

Name.	Section.	Location.	Page.
Steele Roswell Mrs.	41	Evergreen Wood	44
Steele Daniel	12	Greenwood Avenue	59
Stevens and Elmendorf	21	Sunset Lawn	47
Stevenson Robert	59	Western Avenue	86
Stewart Walter D	4	Summer Hill	15
Stickney Moses W	25	Tour	45
Storrs Eliza H. Mrs	89	Tour	112
Strain Joseph	76	Landscape Hill	100
Strong Anthony M	5	Mount Olivet	22
Strong William N	40	Evergreen Path	47
Sumner Alanson and others.	62	Crescent Glade	113
Taber Azor	3	Mount Olivet	23
Talcott S. V. and O. M.	42	Moss Bank Path	26
Ten Eyck Leonard G	43	Spruce Avenue	45
Ten Eyck Jacob H	8	Roseland Way	51
Thacher George H	56	Tour	74
Thomas John	80	Tour	103
Thomas Eliza	74	Arbor Hill	106
Thompson Lemon	41	Forest Avenue	44
Tillinghast William	16	Greenwood Avenue	55
Todd Adam	16	Greenwood Avenue	55
Townsend James	16	Greenwood Avenue	56
Townsend Robert Capt	45	Hemlock Avenue	81
Tremain Lyman	35	Prospect Avenue	28
Tucker William	58	Western Avenue	86
Turnbull John D	43	Tour	45
Turner James	6	Mount Olivet	25
Van Antwerp Family	16	Greenwood Avenue	55
Van Benthuysen Family	5	Mount Olivet	14
Van Buren John Dr.	5	Mount Olivet	20
Van Buren John	62	Crescent Way	89
Vanderpoel Isaac	62	Crescent Way	90
Van Der Werken A. W	16	Greenwood Avenue	56
Van Dyck H. H.	40	Forest Avenue	44
Van Etten James B. Mrs	7	Evergreen Path	25
Van Loon Peter	13	Lawn Avenue	51
Van Rensselaer Solomon Gen	56	Tour	73
Van Rensselaer Family	14	Lawn Avenue	50
Van Schaick Tobias	8	Chapel Grove	11

NAME.	SECTION.	LOCATION.	PAGE.
Van Schaick Stephen.......	5	Mount Olivet...............	16
Van Schaick E..............	5	Mount Olivet...............	19
Van Vechten Abraham......	36	Prospect Avenue...........	29
Van Zandt John.............	52	Western Avenue...........	83
Vaughn Brothers............	60	Crescent Way..............	94
Vernam John.........	62	Crescent Glade.............	113
Viele Augustus Dr....	59	Tour........................	87
Visscher Rosanna...........	16	Tour........................	58
Visscher Family.............	76	Tour........................	100
Vosburgh Isaac W.........	5	Mount Olivet...............	14
Waddell James..............	15	Greenwood Avenue.........	59
Waldron Julia A............	58	Western Avenue...........	85
Walker William J...........	16	Greenwood Avenue.........	58
Walker Frederick W........	80	Pine Grove Avenue.........	104
Wandell Stephen S..........	56	Tour........................	74
Ward John..................	35	Prospect Avenue...........	30
Washburn S. F..............	59	Western Avenue...........	86
Wasson James D............	5	Mount Olivet...............	15
Waterman Smith A........	58	Western Avenue	86
Watson William.............	5	Mount Olivet...............	14
Weed Thurlow..............	3	Chapel Grove..............	18
Weed William G............	16	Highland Water...........	58
Welch B. T. Rev'd.	8	Mount Olivet...............	19
Wells Agur.................	8	Mount Way.................	12
Wells Henry J..............	8	Mount Way....	12
Wendell John I.............	9	Roseland Hill..............	54
Wendell Peter Dr..........	9	Roseland Hill..............	54
Wentz Charles W...........	56	Oak Bough Avenue.........	72
Westerlo Jane..............	77	Landscape Hill.............	103
Wharton William A.........	51	Western Avenue...........	82
Wheeler Abraham M.......	87	Tour........................	109
White Hugh.................	35	Prospect Avenue...........	29
White Family...............	55	Western Avenue...........	84
White Nathaniel B.........	56	Western Avenue...........	84
Whitlock Robert............	5	Mount Olivet...............	23
Wickes Eliphalet...........	5	Mount Olivet...............	16
Wilber Rensselaer..........	94	Meadow Avenue............	112
Wilkinson Jacob............	11	Roseland Hill..............	54
Wilson Jesse P..............	4	Summer Hill...............	15

Name.	Section.	Location.	Page.
Wilson James A	31	Prospect Hill	32
Wilson B	15	Tour	58
Wilson James	8	Tour	61
Wilson Abraham F	56	Western Avenue	84
Williams John	42	Roseleaf Avenue	43
Williamson James Lieut	42	Roseleaf Avenue	43
Wing J. K.	6	Mount Olivet	60
Winne J. heirs of	12	Roseland Way	52
Winne C. H.	15	Lawn Avenue	48
Winslow John F	71	Sunrise Lawn	98
Wiswall Ebenezer	5	Mount Olivet	14
Wood Sarah	5	Mount Olivet	15
Wood Theodore	44	Tour	45
Woodworth David	4	Summer Hill	15
Wooster Benjamin W	25	Primrose Avenue	45
Woolverton G. A. & Chas. B.	13	Lawn Avenue	51
Wyckoff Isaac N. Rev'd	8	Tour	60
Young Hiram	35	Greenleaf Forest	30
Zeh John	44	Roseleaf Avenue	44

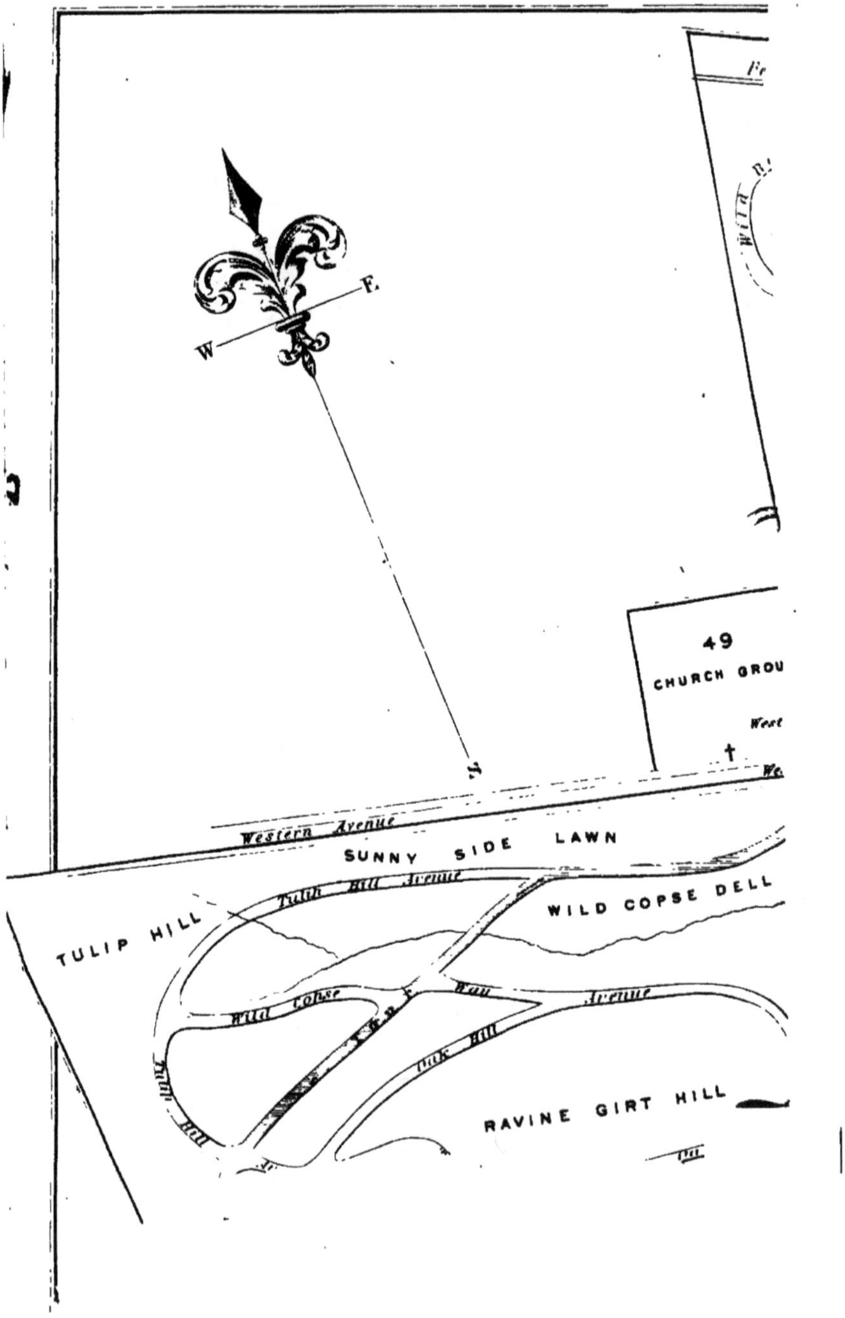

W
E.
49
CHURCH GROU
Western Avenue
SUNNY SIDE LAWN
Tulip Hill Avenue
TULIP HILL
WILD COPSE DELL
Wild Copse
Avenue
Oak Hill
Tulip Hill
RAVINE GIRT HILL

Total Drives 17 Miles